PENGUIN NATURE LIBRARY
General Editor: Edward Hoagland

BIRCH BROWSINGS

John Burroughs (1837–1921) was born near Roxbury, N.Y., the son of Chauncey A. Burroughs, a farmer, and Amy (Kelly) Burroughs. Married in 1857 to Ursula North, Burroughs supported his family first by teaching and then working as a clerk for the Treasury Department in Washington, where he met Walt Whitman, the greatest friend of his life and the subject of his first book. In 1865 the *Atlantic Monthly* published the first of Burroughs's major essays on nature, from which his fame quickly grew. During a writing career of more than sixty years he published more than three hundred essays that eventually helped fill some twenty-seven books, including *Wake-Robin*, *Locusts and Wild Honey*, *Pepacton*, and *Signs and Seasons*. Recognized in his own lifetime as the dean of American nature writers, he traveled much, campaigned against "nature fakers," championed Darwinism, farmed, wrote indefatigably, and numbered among his closest friends Thomas Edison, Theodore Roosevelt, Henry Ford, and John Muir. Burroughs is generally credited with having established the nature essay in its modern form as a literary genre in America.

Bill McKibben is the author of *The Age of Missing Information* and *The End of Nature*. A prolific writer whose work has been translated into fifteen languages, his articles have appeared in *The New Yorker*, *Outside*, and *Natural History*, among other periodicals. He lives in the Adirondack Mountains with his wife and dog.

PENGUIN NATURE LIBRARY

BIRCH BROWSINGS

A John Burroughs Reader

EDITED AND WITH AN INTRODUCTION BY
Bill McKibben

PENGUIN BOOKS

PENGUIN BOOKS
Published by the Penguin Group
Viking Penguin, a division of Penguin Books USA Inc.,
375 Hudson Street, New York, New York 10014, U.S.A.
Penguin Books Ltd, 27 Wrights Lane,
London W8 5TZ, England
Penguin Books Australia Ltd, Ringwood,
Victoria, Australia
Penguin Books Canada Ltd, 10 Alcorn Avenue, Suite 300,
Toronto, Ontario, Canada M4V 3B2
Penguin Books (N.Z.) Ltd, 182–190 Wairau Road,
Auckland 10, New Zealand

Penguin Books Ltd, Registered Offices:
Harmondsworth, Middlesex, England

First published in Penguin Books 1992

1 3 5 7 9 10 8 6 4 2

The text of the essays in this volume is reprinted from the Wake-Robin edition of *The Writings of John Burroughs*, published by William H. Wise & Co. (New York, 1924).
Grateful acknowledgment is made for permission to reprint "Nature Near Home" from the essay "New Gleanings in Old Fields" from *Field and Study*, by John Burroughs. Copyright 1919 by John Burroughs. Copyright 1947 by Julian Burroughs. Reprinted by permission of Houghton Mifflin Company. All rights reserved.

LIBRARY OF CONGRESS CATALOGING IN PUBLICATION DATA
Burroughs, John, 1837–1921.
Birch browsings: a John Burroughs reader/ edited and with an
introduction by Bill McKibben.
p.   cm. — (Penguin nature library)
ISBN 0 14 017.016 2
1. Natural history.   2. Nature stories.   3. Nature in literature.
I. McKibben, Bill.   II. Title.   III. Series.
QH81.B917   1992
508—dc20   92–9466

Printed in the United States of America
Set in Bodoni Book
Designed by Brian Mulligan

THE PENGUIN NATURE LIBRARY

Nature is our widest home. It includes the oceans that provide our rain, the trees that give us air to breathe, the ancestral habitats we shared with countless kinds of animals that now exist only by our sufferance or under our heel.

Until quite recently indeed (as such things go), the whole world was a wilderness in which mankind lived as cannily as deer, overmastering with spears or snares even their woodsmanship and that of other creatures, finding a path wherever wildlife could go. Nature was the central theater of life for everybody's ancestors, not a hideaway where people went to rest and recharge after a hard stint in an urban or suburban arena, and many of us still do swim, hike, fish, birdwatch, sleep on the ground, or paddle a boat on vacation, and will loll like a lizard in the sun any other chance we have. We can't help grinning for at least a moment at the sight of surf, or sunlight on a river meadow, as if remembering in our mind's eye paleolithic pleasures in a home before memories officially began.

It is a thoughtless grin because nature predates "thought." Aristotle was a naturalist, and, nearer to our time, Darwin and Thoreau made of the close observation of bits of nature a lever to examine life in many ways on a large scale. Yet nature writing, despite its basis in science, usually rings with rhapsody as well—a belief that nature is an expression of God.

In this series we are presenting some nature writers of the past century or so, though leaving out great novelists like Turgenev, Melville, Conrad, and Faulkner, who were masters of natural description, and poets such as Homer (who was perhaps the first nature writer, once his words had been transcribed). Nature writing now combines rhapsody with science and connects science with rhapsody. For that reason it is a very special and a nourishing genre.

—Edward Hoagland

CONTENTS

INTRODUCTION

Mount Rainier is the most imposing peak in the Lower Forty-eight, an impossibly large and isolated mountain that rises black and white out of the wet, green rainforest of the Pacific Northwest. The best vantage point for studying the sides of this sublime peak is probably Burroughs Mountain, and thousands of people climb it daily in the summer months.

As I stood there in early September, I found myself thinking how strange it was that this mountain should be named for John Burroughs—strange for two reasons. First, he has almost disappeared from our literary history; it seems hard to believe that only seventy years ago he was popular enough that the people of Washington would name for him a prominent peak he had never visited or written about. And yet they were not alone. In the first two decades of this century he was among our most beloved authors. Presidents and presidential candidates visited his Catskills home; when he traveled across the country with Teddy Roosevelt on one trip, witnesses say it was difficult to tell which man was more popular with the crowds that turned out to greet their train. Nearly every schoolchild read his works in special Houghton-Mifflin educational editions. His work appeared in all the best magazines of his day—for sixty-one years his pieces ran in the *Atlantic*. According to biographer Perry Westbrook, Henry Ford, who kept giving him Model-T automobiles, insisted that his writing was superior to that of any other author who had ever lived. And for all that he has disappeared pretty much without a trace.

But Burroughs Mountain seems strange for another reason, a reason that I think helps explain the nearly total eclipse of Burroughs's reputation. It is a place of rock and ice, of awe-filled and heart-catching views. The bulging, rock-coated tongue of Emmons Glacier spreads out beneath; above are the groaning crevasses and sheer walls that guard the summit. It is the kind of landscape that John Muir loved, and Bob Marshall, and Ansel Adams—and, indeed, most of the other naturalists before and since. Grandeur, awe, spectacle—we have been trained to prize these above all. But Burroughs had little use for the sublime. Instead he filled his many volumes of essays with the most local, small-scale, homey glimpses of nature. When he finally did visit Yosemite, on a rare trip west, he spent his first paragraph extolling the . . . *robin*, "the first I had seen since leaving home. Where the robin is at home, there at home am I." Instead of mountain goats and grizzly bears, he wrote again and again of the chickadee and the woodchuck and the chipmunk. Instead of the vast and unexplored wilderness, he wrote about his native Catskills, where woodlands gave way to pasture and field, where small brooks ran into the placid Hudson. Not great mountains, but round, tree-topped hills. Not geysering Wyoming epiphanies, but gentle and intimate insights. Not untamed wilderness, but half-domesticated forest, slowly healing from the first rounds of logging and mining.

This mild, amiable vision is no longer so fashionable. In their day he and Muir were always "the two Johns," but while the wild and marvelous enthusiasm of Yosemite's poet still ignites our souls, Burroughs's contented and calm appreciations have come to seem quaint. Which is, I think, a shame, for we need them both. Burroughs should be the patron saint of everyone who drives up the Taconic on Friday night for a Berkshires rest, the bard of the birdfeeder. Muir helped us to see and then to save the rocky high places, the aeries where bliss lived. Burroughs could still help us save the woodlots and stream valleys that surround our homes and cottages, for that is where his happiness dwelled. As he confessed, he was never able to bring his "eye to the Alaskan scale," but he was blessed with an unrivaled talent for the familiar.

Besides his concern with nature's more mundane face, several small editorial tics also serve to make Burroughs seem old-fashioned. His fertility (the Riverside edition of his essay collections spans twenty volumes and does not begin to exhaust his output) often leaves him sounding glib and cornball. (Hunters are transformed into nimrods, the fox is invariably Reynard, birds are routinely "songsters," animals who hibernate become "the Rip van Winkles of our brute cast," and a smelly skunk is "Sir Mephitis.") He is forever rating things ("if we take the quality of melody as the test, the wood thrush, hermit thrush, and the veery thrush stand at the head of our list of songsters"), and his judgments are hopelessly parochial: "British trout, by the way, are not so beautiful as our own. They are less brilliantly marked, and have much coarser scales." Also, "our wren-music too is superior to anything of the kind in the Old World," while "our purple finch, or linnet, I am persuaded, ranks far above the English linnet."

This bill of particulars, though, makes him sound like a sort of rusticating Andy Rooney, when in fact he was remarkably open to the new and challenging. Burroughs's first book, for instance, was also the first book written about Walt Whitman, and throughout his career he again and again championed the poet, a dear friend, in the battles against obscurity and then condemnation. He was the same sort of midwife for Darwin, repeatedly defending what were still controversial ideas before his vast public. His adaptability was stunning: he worked in Washington during the Civil War and his last collection was published after World War I, but though few lifetimes have seen such tectonic intellectual shifts, he was rarely fazed. Most remarkably, perhaps, he defended emerging scientific truths but skipped the stage of infatuation with the purely rational. He kept his sense of the natural world's wonder when all around the claims of reason or fulminating religion were felling lesser essayists. "I think that if I could be persuaded, as my fathers were, that the world was made in six days, by the fiat of a supernatural power, I should soon lose my interest in it," he wrote. But also this: "We may know an animal in the light of all the many tests that laboratory experimentation throws on it . . . we stone it, we electrocute it, we freeze it, we burn it . . . and yet not really know it at all. We are not content to know what an animal knows naturally, we want to know what it knows unnaturally." And also this: "The love of nature is a different thing from the love of science. . . . Without a sense of the unknown and unknowable, life is flat and barren." These may not seem such revolutionary sentiments, but our culture is still groping toward them, toward the place where Burroughs had serenely arrived in 1910. He was that rarest of birds, a writer at ease with the change around him and yet not its slave, comfortable with his time but not denying the sweetness of the past.

Still and all, it was not his philosophizing that endeared him to his public. "I am quite certain," he wrote, "that the majority of my readers would have me always stick to natural history themes." And he was right, for he was without peer as an observer. Most of us, out for a walk, soon tune out much of the world around: unless we're listening specifically for them, the bird calls do not break through the soundtrack of our thoughts. But Burroughs not only heard, he recounted so effectively that one's subconscious memory is jogged. Describing the song of the hermit thrush he writes:

> It is very simple and I can hardly tell the secret of its charm. 'O spheral, spheral!' he seems to say; 'O holy, holy! O clear away, clear away! O clear up, clear up!' interspersed with the finest trills and the most delicate preludes. It is not a proud, gorgeous strain, like the tanager's or the grosbeak's; suggests no passion or emotion—nothing personal—but seems to be the voice of that calm, sweet solemnity one attains to in his best moments.

His technique captures not only the sound of a call but the spirit—accurately, at least for the species I know. He insists, for instance, that the bobolink is unequaled in "the qualities of hilarity and musical tintinnabulation," and he renders its song as "Ha! ha! ha! I must have my fun, Miss Silverthimble, thimble, thimble, if I break every heart in the meadow, see,

see, see!" As for the meadowlark, "what a twang there is about this bird, and what vigor! It smacks of the soil. . . . 'Spring o' the year! spring o' the year!' it says, with a long-drawn breath, a little plaintive, but not complaining or melancholy." And his talent does not end with birds: "the cow has at least four tones or lows," he reports, including "the long, sonorous volley she lets off on the hills or in the yard, or along the highway, and which seems to be expressive of a kind of unrest and vague longing."

Such precision required long hours of concentration. "The casual glances or the admiring glances that we cast upon nature do not go very far in making us acquainted with her real ways," writes Burroughs, who waged the only real battle of his career with the "nature-fakers," competing essayists who were forever producing charming reports of, say, birds who tied knots in the strings that hung from their nests so the ends wouldn't fray. (President Roosevelt joined him in the campaign against the sham naturalists, and together they vanquished the opposition.) Instead, Burroughs relied on steady and patient observation, returning again and again to any behavior he couldn't understand. On finding piles of earth in his field, for instance, he staked them out with the zeal of a cop until he determined they were made by chipmunks building their nests. He would count the buckwheat seeds in their winter caches (before replacing them) and mark down for another day his remaining doubts: do female chipmunks dig their own dens or find abandoned ones? He followed mice trails, left out ripe plums to see how the squirrels would handle them, tracked bees miles through the woods to their hives, spent days walking through England stopping everyone who passed to ask if they had recently heard a nightingale sing, and if so would they take

him to the spot. ("If all the people of whom I inquired for
nightingales in England could have been together and compared notes, they probably would not have been long in deciding that there was at least one crazy American abroad.")
These investigations were not conducted scientifically—he
never designed experiments or published papers. They were,
instead, an excuse to immerse himself in the harmony of the
world around him, a harmony he felt profoundly.

And a harmony in which people played a part. Naturalists
have sometimes tended to be cranks. Many went to the woods
or the deserts or the mountains to escape people; landscapes
altered by human beings depressed them, while wilderness
produced elation. And this crankiness has served useful ends:
there are vast areas preserved today, and dozens of species
alive, because of Muir and the rest. Burroughs, however, was
constitutionally different—mild, not fierce. Many have praised
the grizzly and the elk, but few naturalists save Burroughs have
hymned the cow.

> Into what artistic groups they naturally fall, what pictures
> of peace and plenty they produce . . . she is the cause
> of tranquil if not of great thoughts in the lookers-on, and
> that is enough. Tranquility attends her wherever she goes;
> it beams from her eyes and lingers in her footsteps.

He adores as well the cow's owner, working hard to create
better pasture:

> Last summer I saw him take enough stones and rocks
> from a three-acre field to build quite a fortress, and land
> whose slumbers had never been disturbed with the plough
> was soon knee-high with Hungarian grass. How one likes

to see a permanent betterment of the land like that!—
piles of renegade stone and rock. It is such things that
make the country richer.

Our fascination with the grand, the violent, the awesome,
the pure, the wild—a fascination I share—can be treacherous.
Valuing spectacle, I find myself rushing up the mountain for
the view. And of course the "ordinary" nature I pass along the
way makes up the world. For every Grand Canyon there are a
million drainages between low hills, a million small creeks.
Burroughs is the Powell of these gulches: his great solo voyage
in twenty volumes is down the east or Pepacton branch of the
Delaware, a placid stream if ever there was one. And yet its
headwaters are too wild for him. He complains not only about
a farmwife whom he suspects of skimming the milk before she
sells it to him ("its blueness infected my spirits") but also about
the fallen trees blocking the river and the willows along the
shore "where I would lose my hat."

> The loneliness of the river, too, unlike that of the fields
> and woods, to which I was more accustomed, oppressed
> me. . . . The long, unpeopled vistas ahead; the still, dark
> eddies; the endless monotone and soliloquy of the stream
> . . . the trees and willows and alders that hemmed you
> in on either side, and hid the fields and the farmhouses
> and the road that ran nearby—these things and others
> aided the skimmed milk to cast a gloom over my spirits.

As he meanders down the river for the next five days, though,
he starts to run into more people: an old fisherman, and some
schoolgirls "with skirts amazingly abbreviated, wading and
playing in the water," and a farmwife from whom he tries to

buy more milk (" 'What do you want to do with it?' [she asked] with an anxious tone, as if I might want to blow up something or burn her barns with it"), and two boys on the way home from running away, and some hunters, and a schoolmarm, and a crew of railroad workers on a handcar. After a week or so, "my voyage ended at Hancock, and was crowned by a few idyllic days with some friends at their cottage near Lake Oquaga."

Whether naturalists like it or not, Burroughs's experience of the world outdoors will always dominate. This continent will never again be one vast wilderness—we are not, as some deep ecologists have suggested, going to construct a few great cities on either shore and leave the interior to the buffalo. The best we can hope for—and we should work for no less—is the preservation of the wild acres that still exist, and their expansion around the edges until they are ecologically secure and sensible. Which means that most of the nation will remain neither urban nor wild but somewhere in between. Learning to appreciate that middle kingdom should be one of our chief goals—it's why we need Burroughs as badly as Muir. As his vast popularity demonstrated, he figured out a language for making others treasure the small spectacles of nature—he articulated the mute delight that people have always taken in their surroundings. He lovingly chronicled the change of the seasons, for instance, noting with a country man's precision the slight but significant shifts that mark the wheel as she turns. It is usually late in April, he writes,

> when we observe the first quickening of the earth. The waters have subsided, the roads have become dry, the sunshine has grown strong and its warmth has penetrated

the sod. . . . The warm, moist places, the places that
have had the wash of some building or of the road . . .
how quickly the turf awakens there and shows the tender
green. . . . As the later snows lay in patches here and
there, so now the earliest verdure is spread irregularly
over the landscape, and is especially marked on certain
slopes, as if it had blown over from the other side and
lodged there. . . . The full charm of this April landscape
is not brought out until the later afternoon. . . . When
the faint, four-o'clock shadows begin to come, and we
look through the green vistas, and along the farm lanes
toward the west, or out across long stretches above which
spring seems fairly hovering, just ready to alight, and
notice the teams slowly plowing the brightened mould-
board gleaming in the sun now and then—it is at such
times we feel its fresh, delicate attention the most.

   This contentedness can be overdone, and Burroughs had
a tendency to stand gazing with bovine nonchalance at environmental destruction he should have been able to foresee: he
was best buddies not only with Ford but with Edison and
Firestone and he seems not to have given a thought to the
havoc their inventions might produce. Always an optimist ("the
fuel in the earth will be exhausted in a thousand or more years,
and its mineral wealth, but man will find substitutes for these
in the winds, the waves, the sun's heat, and so forth"), he
came to terms with the popular too easily—save for his battle
with the nature-fakers, he is almost never critical of anyone
or anything in his books.
   Still, his moderation, his mellow calm, and most of all his
seductive descriptions of the beauty and order around his Cats-

kills study should make him a vital part of the environmental movement. What Jefferson argued for in political terms, what Wendell Berry has embraced for its moral power, he loved for its aesthetic value. "Read correctly the moral of the solar system—this harmony, this balance, this compensation—and there is no deeper lesson to be heard," he insisted, an argument from ecological bedrock that preceded by some decades the popularization of ecology. Most of us will never experience firsthand Muir's bliss at a summer in the unpeopled Sierras, or follow Bob Marshall into the unexplored Brooks Range. But most of us can learn the lessons of chipmunks and bluebirds, which Burroughs proved were also windows on the infinite wonder. On Burroughs Mountain, if Rainier is in the clouds, we can turn our backs on the great peak and hunt instead for a glimpse of the marmot, a sort of alpine woodchuck, as it pops in and out of the rocks. "Scenery may be too fine or too grand and imposing for one's daily and hourly view. It tires after a while. It demands a mood that comes to you at intervals," he wrote. "In some things, the half is more often satisfying than the whole."

—Bill McKibben

BIRCH
BROWSINGS

BIRCH BROWSINGS

The region of which I am about to speak lies in the southern part of the State of New York, and comprises parts of three counties,—Ulster, Sullivan, and Delaware. It is drained by tributaries of both the Hudson and Delaware, and, next to the Adirondack section, contains more wild land than any other tract in the State. The mountains which traverse it, and impart to it its severe northern climate, belong properly to the Catskill range. On some maps of the State they are called the Pine Mountains, though with obvious local impropriety, as pine, so far as I have observed, is nowhere found upon them. "Birch Mountains" would be a more characteristic name, as on their summits birch is the prevailing tree. They are the natural home of the black and yellow birch, which grow here to unusual size. On their sides beech and maple abound; while, mantling their lower slopes and darkening the valleys, hemlock formerly enticed the lumberman and tanner. Except in remote or inaccessible localities, the latter tree is now almost never found. In Shandaken and along the Esopus it is about the only product the country yielded,

1

or is likely to yield. Tanneries by the score have arisen and flourished upon the bark, and some of them still remain. Passing through that region the present season, I saw that the few patches of hemlock that still lingered high up on the sides of the mountains were being felled and peeled, the fresh white boles of the trees, just stripped of their bark, being visible a long distance.

Among these mountains there are no sharp peaks, or abrupt declivities, as in a volcanic region, but long, uniform ranges, heavily timbered to their summits, and delighting the eye with vast, undulating horizon lines. Looking south from the heights about the head of the Delaware, one sees, twenty miles away, a continual succession of blue ranges, one behind the other. If a few large trees are missing on the sky line, one can see the break a long distance off.

Approaching this region from the Hudson River side, you cross a rough, rolling stretch of country, skirting the base of the Catskills, which from a point near Saugerties sweep inland; after a drive of a few hours you are within the shadow of a high, bold mountain, which forms a sort of butt-end to this part of the range, and which is simply called High Point. To the east and southeast it slopes down rapidly to the plain, and looks defiance toward the Hudson, twenty miles distant; in the rear of it, and radiating from it west and northwest, are numerous smaller ranges, backing up, as it were, this haughty chief.

From this point through to Pennsylvania, a distance of nearly one hundred miles, stretches the tract of which I speak. It is a belt of country from twenty to thirty miles wide, bleak and wild, and but sparsely settled. The traveler on the New York and Erie Railroad gets a glimpse of it.

Many cold, rapid trout streams, which flow to all points of the compass, have their source in the small lakes and copious mountain springs of this region. The names of some of them are Mill Brook, Dry Brook, Willewemack, Beaver Kill, Elk Bush Kill, Panther Kill, Neversink, Big Ingin, and Callikoon. Beaver Kill is the main outlet on the west. It joins the Delaware in the wilds of Hancock. The Neversink lays open the region to the south, and also joins the Delaware. To the east, various Kills unite with the Big Ingin to form the Esopus, which flows into the Hudson. Dry Brook and Mill Brook, both famous trout streams, from twelve to fifteen miles long, find their way into the Delaware.

The east or Pepacton branch of the Delaware itself takes its rise near here in a deep pass between the mountains. I have many times drunk at a copious spring by the roadside, where the infant river first sees the light. A few yards beyond, the water flows the other way, directing its course through the Bear Kill and Schoharie Kill into the Mohawk.

Such game and wild animals as still linger in the State are found in this region. Bears occasionally make havoc among the sheep. The clearings at the head of a valley are oftenest the scene of their depredations.

Wild pigeons, in immense numbers, used to breed regularly in the valley of the Big Ingin and about the head of the Neversink. The treetops for miles were full of their nests, while the going and coming of the old birds kept up a constant din. But the gunners soon got wind of it, and from far and near were wont to pour in during the spring, and to slaughter both old and young. This practice soon had the effect of driving the pigeons all away, and now only a few pairs breed in these woods.

Deer are still met with, though they are becoming scarcer every year. Last winter near seventy head were killed on the Beaver Kill alone. I heard of one wretch, who, finding the deer snowbound, walked up to them on his snowshoes, and one morning before breakfast slaughtered six, leaving their carcasses where they fell. There are traditions of persons having been smitten blind or senseless when about to commit some heinous offense, but the fact that this villain escaped without some such visitation throws discredit on all such stories.

The great attraction, however, of this region, is the brook trout, with which the streams and lakes abound. The water is of excessive coldness, the thermometer indicating 44° and 45° in the springs, and 47° or 48° in the smaller streams. The trout are generally small, but in the more remote branches their number is very great. In such localities the fish are quite black, but in the lakes they are of a lustre and brilliancy impossible to describe.

These waters have been much visited of late years by fishing parties, and the name of Beaver Kill is now a potent word among New York sportsmen.

One lake, in the wilds of Callikoon, abounds in a peculiar species of white sucker, which is of excellent quality. It is taken only in spring, during the spawning season, at the time "when the leaves are as big as a chipmunk's ears." The fish run up the small streams and inlets, beginning at nightfall, and continuing till the channel is literally packed with them, and every inch of space is occupied. The fishermen pounce upon them at such times, and scoop them up by the bushel, usually wading right into the living mass and landing the fish with their hands. A small party will often secure in this manner a wagon load of fish. Certain conditions of the weather, as a

warm south or southwest wind, are considered most favorable
for the fish to run.

Though familiar all my life with the outskirts of this region,
I have only twice dipped into its wilder portions. Once in 1860
a friend and myself traced the Beaver Kill to its source, and
encamped by Balsam Lake. A cold and protracted rainstorm
coming on, we were obliged to leave the woods before we were
ready. Neither of us will soon forget that tramp by an unknown
route over the mountains, incumbered as we were with a
hundred and one superfluities which we had foolishly brought
along to solace ourselves with in the woods; nor that halt on
the summit, where we cooked and ate our fish in a drizzling
rain; nor, again, that rude log house, with its sweet hospitality,
which we reached just at nightfall on Mill Brook.

In 1868 a party of three of us set out for a brief trouting
excursion to a body of water called Thomas's Lake, situated
in the same chain of mountains. On this excursion, more particularly than on any other I have ever undertaken, I was taught
how poor an Indian I should make, and what a ridiculous figure
a party of men may cut in the woods when the way is uncertain
and the mountains high.

We left our team at a farmhouse near the head of the Mill
Brook, one June afternoon, and with knapsacks on our shoulders struck into the woods at the base of the mountain, hoping
to cross the range that intervened between us and the lake by
sunset. We engaged a good-natured but rather indolent young
man, who happened to be stopping at the house, and who had
carried a knapsack in the Union armies, to pilot us a couple
of miles into the woods so as to guard against any mistakes at
the outset. It seemed the easiest thing in the world to find the
lake. The lay of the land was so simple, according to accounts,

that I felt sure I could go to it in the dark. "Go up this little
brook to its source on the side of the mountain," they said.
"The valley that contains the lake heads directly on the other
side." What could be easier! But on a little further inquiry,
they said we should "bear well to the left" when we reached
the top of the mountain. This opened the doors again; "bearing
well to the left" was an uncertain performance in strange woods.
We might bear so well to the left that it would bring us ill.
But why bear to the left at all, if the lake was directly opposite?
Well, not quite opposite; a little to the left. There were two or
three other valleys that headed in near there. We could easily
find the right one. But to make assurance doubly sure, we
engaged a guide, as stated, to give us a good start, and go
with us beyond the bearing-to-the-left point. He had been to
the lake the winter before and knew the way. Our course, the
first half hour, was along an obscure wood-road which had been
used for drawing ash logs off the mountain in winter. There
was some hemlock, but more maple and birch. The woods were
dense and free from underbrush, the ascent gradual. Most of
the way we kept the voice of the creek in our ear on the right.
I approached it once, and found it swarming with trout. The
water was as cold as one ever need wish. After a while the
ascent grew steeper, the creek became a mere rill that issued
from beneath loose, moss-covered rocks and stones, and with
much labor and puffing we drew ourselves up the rugged de-
clivity. Every mountain has its steepest point, which is usually
near the summit, in keeping, I suppose, with the providence
that makes the darkest hour just before day. It is steep, steeper,
steepest, till you emerge on the smooth level or gently rounded
space at the top, which the old ice-gods polished off so long
ago.

We found this mountain had a hollow in its back where the ground was soft and swampy. Some gigantic ferns, which we passed through, came nearly to our shoulders. We passed also several patches of swamp honeysuckles, red with blossoms.

Our guide at length paused on a big rock where the land began to dip down the other way, and concluded that he had gone far enough, and that we would now have no difficulty in finding the lake. "It must lie right down there," he said, pointing with his hand. But it was plain that he was not quite sure in his own mind. He had several times wavered in his course, and had shown considerable embarrassment when bearing to the left across the summit. Still we thought little of it. We were full of confidence, and, bidding him adieu, plunged down the mountain-side, following a spring run that we had no doubt led to the lake.

In these woods, which had a southeastern exposure, I first began to notice the wood thrush. In coming up the other side I had not seen a feather of any kind, or heard a note. Now the golden *trillide-de* of the wood thrush sounded through the silent woods. While looking for a fish-pole about half way down the mountain, I saw a thrush's nest in a little sapling about ten feet from the ground.

After continuing our descent till our only guide, the spring run, became quite a trout brook, and its tiny murmur a loud brawl, we began to peer anxiously through the trees for a glimpse of the lake, or for some conformation of the land that would indicate its proximity. An object which we vaguely discerned in looking under the near trees and over the more distant ones proved, on further inspection, to be a patch of plowed ground. Presently we made out a burnt fallow near it. This was a wet blanket to our enthusiasm. No lake, no sport, no trout for supper that night. The rather indolent young man had either played us a trick, or, as seemed more likely, had missed the way. We were particularly anxious to be at the lake between sundown and dark, as at that time the trout jump most freely.

Pushing on, we soon emerged into a stumpy field, at the head of a steep valley, which swept around toward the west. About two hundred rods below us was a rude log house, with smoke issuing from the chimney. A boy came out and moved toward the spring with a pail in his hand. We shouted to him, when he turned and ran back into the house without pausing to reply. In a moment the whole family hastily rushed into the yard, and turned their faces toward us. If we had come down their chimney, they could not have seemed more astonished. Not making out what they said, I went down to the house, and learned to my chagrin that we were still on the Mill Brook side, having crossed only a spur of the mountain. We had not borne sufficiently to the left, so that the main range, which, at the point of crossing, suddenly breaks off to the southeast, still intervened between us and the lake. We were about five miles, as the water runs, from the point of starting, and over two from the lake. We must go directly back to the top of the range where the guide had left us, and then, by keeping well to the left, we would soon come to a line of marked trees, which would lead us to the lake. So, turning upon our trail, we doggedly began the work of undoing what we had just done, —in all cases a disagreeable task, in this case a very laborious one also. It was after sunset when we turned back, and before we had got half way up the mountain it began to be quite dark. We were often obliged to rest our packs against trees and take breath, which made our progress slow. Finally a halt was called, beside an immense flat rock which had paused in its slide down the mountain, and we prepared to encamp for the night. A fire was built, the rock cleared off, a small ration of bread served out, our accoutrements hung up out of the way of the hedgehogs that were supposed to infest the locality, and then we disposed ourselves for sleep. If the owls or porcupines (and I think I heard one of the latter in the middle of the night) reconnoitred our camp, they saw a buffalo robe spread upon a rock, with three old felt hats arranged on one side, and three pairs of sorry-looking cowhide boots protruding from the other.

When we lay down, there was apparently not a mosquito in the woods; but the "no-see-ems," as Thoreau's Indian aptly named the midges, soon found us out, and after the fire had gone down annoyed us much. My hands and wrists suddenly began to smart and itch in a most unaccountable manner. My first thought was that they had been poisoned in some way. Then the smarting extended to my neck and face, even to my scalp, when I began to suspect what was the matter. So, wrapping myself up more thoroughly, and stowing my hands away as best I could, I tried to sleep, being some time behind my companions, who appeared not to mind the "no-see-ems." I was further annoyed by some little irregularity on my side of the couch. The chambermaid had not beaten it up well. One huge lump refused to be mollified, and each attempt to adapt it to some natural hollow in my own body brought only a moment's relief. But at last I got the better of this also and slept. Late in the night I woke up, just in time to hear a golden-crowned thrush sing in a tree near by. It sang as loud and cheerily as at midday, and I thought myself after all, quite in luck. Birds occasionally sing at night, just as the cock crows. I have heard the hairbird, and the note of the kingbird; and the ruffed grouse frequently drums at night.

At the first faint signs of day a wood thrush sang, a few rods below us. Then after a little delay, as the gray light began to grow around, thrushes broke out in full song in all parts of the woods. I thought I had never before heard them sing so sweetly. Such a leisurely, golden chant!—it consoled us for all we had undergone. It was the first thing in order,—the worms were safe till after this morning chorus. I judged that the birds roosted but a few feet from the ground. In fact, a bird in all cases roosts where it builds, and the wood thrush occupies, as it were, the first story of the woods.

There is something singular about the distribution of the wood thrushes. At an earlier stage of my observations I should have been much surprised at finding them in these woods. Indeed, I had stated in print on two occasions that the wood thrush was not found in the higher lands of the Catskills, but that the hermit thrush and the veery, or Wilson's thrush, were common. It turns out that this statement is only half true. The wood thrush is found also, but is much more rare and secluded in its habits than either of the others, being seen only during the breeding season on remote mountains, and then only on their eastern and southern slopes. I have never yet in this region found the bird spending the season in the near and familiar woods, which is directly contrary to observations I have made in other parts of the State. So different are the habits of birds in different localities.

As soon as it was fairly light we were up and ready to resume our march. A small bit of bread-and-butter and a swallow or two of whiskey was all we had for breakfast that morning.

Our supply of each was very limited, and we were anxious to save a little of both, to relieve the diet of trout to which we looked forward.

At an early hour we reached the rock where we had parted with the guide, and looked around us into the dense, trackless woods with many misgivings. To strike out now on our own hook, where the way was so blind and after the experience we had just had, was a step not to be carelessly taken. The tops of these mountains are so broad, and a short distance in the woods seems so far, that one is by no means master of the situation after reaching the summit. And then there are so many spurs and offshoots and changes of direction, added to the impossibility of making any generalization by the aid of the eye, that before one is aware of it he is very wide of his mark.

I remembered now that a young farmer of my acquaintance had told me how he had made a long day's march through the heart of this region, without path or guide of any kind, and had hit his mark squarely. He had been barkpeeling in Callikoon,—a famous country for bark,—and, having got enough of it, he desired to reach his home on Dry Brook without making the usual circuitous journey between the two places. To do this necessitated a march of ten or twelve miles across several ranges of mountains and through an unbroken forest, —a hazardous undertaking in which no one would join him. Even the old hunters who were familiar with the ground dissuaded him and predicted the failure of his enterprise. But having made up his mind, he possessed himself thoroughly of the topography of the country from the aforesaid hunters, shouldered his axe, and set out, holding a straight course through the woods, and turning aside for neither swamps, streams, nor mountains. When he paused to rest he would mark some object ahead of him with his eye, in order that on getting up again he might not deviate from his course. His directors had told him of a hunter's cabin about midway on his route, which if he struck he might be sure he was right. About noon this cabin was reached, and at sunset he emerged at the head of Dry Brook.

After looking in vain for the line of marked trees, we moved off to the left in a doubtful, hesitating manner, keeping on the highest ground and blazing the trees as we went. We were afraid to go down hill, lest we should descend too soon; our vantage-ground was high ground. A thick fog coming on, we were more bewildered than ever. Still we pressed forward, climbing up ledges and wading through ferns for about two hours, when we paused by a spring that issued from beneath an immense wall of rock that belted the highest part of the mountain. There was quite a broad plateau here, and the birch wood was very dense, and the trees of unusual size.

After resting and exchanging opinions, we all concluded that it was best not to continue our search incumbered as we were; but we were not willing to abandon it altogether, and I proposed to my companions to leave them beside the spring with our traps, while I made one thorough and final effort to find the lake. If I succeeded and desired them to come forward, I was to fire my gun three times; if I failed and wished to return, I would fire it twice, they of course responding.

So, filling my canteen from the spring, I set out again, taking the spring run for my guide. Before I had followed it two hundred yards it sank into the ground at my feet. I had half a mind to be superstitious and to believe that we were under a spell, since our guides played us such tricks. However,

I determined to put the matter to a further test, and struck out boldly to the left. This seemed to be the keyword,—to the left, to the left. The fog had now lifted, so that I could form a better idea of the lay of the land. Twice I looked down the steep sides of the mountain, sorely tempted to risk a plunge. Still I hesitated and kept along on the brink. As I stood on a rock deliberating, I heard a crackling of the brush, like the tread of some large game, on a plateau below me. Suspecting the truth of the case, I moved stealthily down, and found a herd of young cattle leisurely browsing. We had several times crossed their trail, and had seen that morning a level, grassy place on the top of the mountain, where they had passed the night. Instead of being frightened, as I had expected, they seemed greatly delighted, and gathered around me as if to inquire the tidings from the outer world,—perhaps the quotations of the cattle market. They came up to me, and eagerly licked my hand, clothes, and gun. Salt was what they were after, and they were ready to swallow anything that contained the smallest percentage of it. They were mostly yearlings and as sleek as moles. They had a very gamy look. We were afterwards told that, in the spring, the farmers round about turn into these woods their young cattle, which do not come out again till fall. They are then in good condition,—not fat, like grass-fed cattle, but trim and supple, like deer. Once a month the owner hunts them up and salts them. They have their beats, and seldom wander beyond well-defined limits. It was interesting to see them feed. They browsed on the low limbs and bushes, and on the various plants, munching at everything without any apparent discrimination.

They attempted to follow me, but I escaped them by clambering down some steep rocks. I now found myself gradually edging down the side of the mountain, keeping around it in a spiral manner, and scanning the woods and the shape of the ground for some encouraging hint or sign. Finally the woods became more open, and the descent less rapid. The trees were remarkably straight and uniform in size. Black birches, the first I had seen, were very numerous. I felt encouraged. Listening attentively, I caught, from a breeze just lifting the drooping leaves, a sound that I willingly believed was made by a bullfrog. On this hint, I tore down through the woods at my highest speed. Then I paused and listened again. This time there was no mistaking it; it was the sound of frogs. Much elated, I rushed on. By and by I could hear them as I ran. *Pthrung, pthrung*, croaked the old ones; *pug, pug*, shrilly joined in the smaller fry.

Then I caught, through the lower trees, a gleam of blue, which I first thought was distant sky. A second look and I knew it to be water, and in a moment more I stepped from the woods and stood upon the shore of the lake. I exulted silently. There it was at last, sparkling in the morning sun, and as beautiful as a dream. It was so good to come upon such open space and such bright hues, after wandering in the dim, dense woods! The eye is as delighted as an escaped bird, and darts gleefully from point to point.

The lake was a long oval, scarcely more than a mile in circumference, with evenly wooded shores, which rose gradually on all sides. After contemplating the scene for a moment, I stepped back into the woods, and, loading my gun as heavily as I dared, discharged it three times. The reports seemed to fill all the mountains with sound. The frogs quickly hushed, and I listened for the response. But no response came. Then I tried again and again, but without evoking an answer. One of my companions, however, who had climbed to the top of the high rocks in the rear of the spring, thought he heard faintly one report. It seemed an immense distance below him, and far around under the mountain. I knew I had come a long way, and hardly expected to be able to communicate with my companions in the manner agreed upon. I therefore started back, choosing my course without any reference to the circuitous route by which I had come, and loading heavily and firing at intervals. I must have aroused many long-dormant echoes from a Rip Van Winkle sleep. As my powder got low, I fired and halloed alternately, till I came near splitting both my throat and gun. Finally, after I had begun to have a very ugly feeling of alarm and disappointment, and to cast about vaguely for some course to pursue in the emergency that seemed near at hand,—namely, the loss of my companions now I had found the lake,—a favoring breeze brought me the last echo of a response. I rejoined with spirit, and hastened with all speed in the direction whence the sound had come, but, after repeated trials, failed to elicit another answering sound. This filled me with apprehension again. I feared that my friends had been misled by the reverberations, and I pictured them to myself hastening in the opposite direction. Paying little attention to my course, but paying dearly for my carelessness afterward, I rushed forward to undeceive them. But they had not been deceived, and in a few moments an answering shout revealed them near at hand. I heard their tramp, the bushes parted, and we three met again.

In answer to their eager inquiries, I assured them that I had seen the lake, that it was at the foot of the mountain, and that we could not miss it if we kept straight down from where we then were.

My clothes were soaked with perspiration, but I shouldered my knapsack with alacrity, and we began the descent. I noticed that the woods were much thicker, and had quite a different look from those I had passed through, but thought nothing of it, as I expected to strike the lake near its head, whereas I had before come out at its foot. We had not gone far when we crossed a line of marked trees, which my companions were disposed to follow. It intersected our course nearly at right angles, and kept along and up the side of the mountain. My impression was that it led up from the lake, and that by keeping our own course we should reach the lake sooner than if we followed this line.

About half way down the mountain, we could see through the interstices the opposite slope. I encouraged my comrades by telling them that the lake was between us and that, and not more than half a mile distant. We soon reached the bottom, where we found a small stream and quite an extensive alder swamp, evidently the ancient bed of a lake. I explained to my half-vexed and half-incredulous companions that we were probably above the lake, and that this stream must lead to it. "Follow it," they said; "we will wait here till we hear from you."

So I went on, more than ever disposed to believe that we were under a spell, and that the lake had slipped from my grasp after all. Seeing no favorable sign as I went forward, I laid down my accoutrements, and climbed a decayed beech that leaned out over the swamp and promised a good view from the top. As I stretched myself up to look around from the highest attainable branch, there was suddenly a loud crack at the root. With a celerity that would at least have done credit to a bear, I regained the ground, having caught but a momentary glimpse of the country, but enough to convince me no lake was near. Leaving all incumbrances here but my gun, I still pressed on, loath to be thus baffled. After floundering through another alder swamp for nearly half a mile, I flattered myself that I was close on to the lake. I caught sight of a low spur of the mountain sweeping around like a half-extended arm, and I fondly imagined that within its clasp was the object of my search. But I found only more alder swamp. After this region was cleared, the creek began to descend the mountain very rapidly. Its banks became high and narrow, and it went whirling away with a sound that seemed to my ears like a burst of ironical laughter. I turned back with a feeling of mingled disgust, shame, and vexation. In fact I was almost sick, and when I reached my companions, after an absence of nearly two hours, hungry, fatigued, and disheartened, I would have sold my interest in Thomas's Lake at a very low figure. For the first time, I heartily wished myself well out of the woods. Thomas might keep his lake, and the enchanters guard his possession! I doubted if he had ever found it the second time, or if any one else ever had.

My companions, who were quite fresh, and who had not felt the strain of baffled purpose as I had, assumed a more encouraging tone. After I had rested a while, and partaken sparingly of the bread and whiskey, which in such an emergency is a great improvement on bread and water, I agreed to their proposition that we should make another attempt. As if to reassure us, a robin sounded his cheery call near by, and the winter wren, the first I had heard in these woods, set his music-box going, which fairly ran over with fine, gushing, lyrical sounds. There can be no doubt but this bird is one of our finest songsters. If it would only thrive and sing well when caged, like the canary, how far it would surpass that bird! It has all the vivacity and versatility of the canary, without any of its shrillness. Its song is indeed a little cascade of melody.

We again retraced our steps, rolling the stone, as it were, back up the mountain, determined to commit ourselves to the line of marked trees. These we finally reached, and, after exploring the country to the right, saw that bearing to the left was still the order. The trail led up over a gentle rise of ground, and in less than twenty minutes we were in the woods I had passed through when I found the lake. The error I had made was then plain; we had come off the mountain a few paces too far to the right, and so had passed down on the wrong side of the ridge, into what we afterwards learned was the valley of Alder Creek.

We now made good time, and before many minutes I again saw the mimic sky glance through the trees. As we approached the lake a solitary woodchuck, the first wild animal we had seen since entering the woods, sat crouched upon the root of a tree a few feet from the water, apparently completely nonplussed by the unexpected appearance of danger on the land side. All retreat was cut off, and he looked his fate in the face without flinching. I slaughtered him just as a savage would have done, and from the same motive,—I wanted his carcass to eat.

The mid-afternoon sun was now shining upon the lake, and a low, steady breeze drove the little waves rocking to the shore. A herd of cattle were browsing on the other side, and the bell of the leader sounded across the water. In these solitudes its clang was wild and musical.

To try the trout was the first thing in order. On a rude raft of logs which we found moored at the shore, and which with two aboard shipped about a foot of water, we floated out and wet our first fly in Thomas's Lake; but the trout refused to jump, and, to be frank, not more than a dozen and a half were caught during our stay. Only a week previous, a party of three had taken in a few hours all the fish they could carry out of the woods, and had nearly surfeited their neighbors with trout. But from some cause they now refused to rise, or to touch any kind of bait: so we fell to catching the sunfish, which were small but very abundant. Their nests were all along shore. A space about the size of a breakfast-plate was cleared of sediment and decayed vegetable matter, revealing the pebbly bottom, fresh and bright, with one or two fish suspended over the centre of it, keeping watch and ward. If an intruder approached, they would dart at him spitefully. These fish have the air of bantam cocks, and, with their sharp, prickly fins and spines and scaly sides, must be ugly customers in a hand-to-hand encounter with other finny warriors. To a hungry man they look about as unpromising as hemlock slivers, so thorny and thin are they; yet there is sweet meat in them, as we found that day.

Much refreshed, I set out with the sun low in the west to explore the outlet of the lake and try for trout there, while my companions made further trials in the lake itself. The outlet, as is usual in bodies of water of this kind, was very gentle and private. The stream, six or eight feet wide, flowed silently and evenly along for a distance of three or four rods, when it suddenly, as if conscious of its freedom, took a leap down some rocks. Thence, as far as I followed it, its descent was very rapid through a continuous succession of brief falls like so many steps down the mountain. Its appearance promised more trout than I found, though I returned to camp with a very respectable string.

Toward sunset I went round to explore the inlet, and found that as usual the stream wound leisurely through marshy ground. The water being much colder than in the outlet, the trout were more plentiful. As I was picking my way over the miry ground and through the rank growths, a ruffed grouse hopped up on a fallen branch a few paces before me, and, jerking his tail, threatened to take flight. But as I was at that moment gunless and remained stationary, he presently jumped down and walked away.

A seeker of birds, and ever on the alert for some new acquaintance, my attention was arrested, on first entering the swamp, by a bright, lively song, or warble, that issued from the branches overhead, and that was entirely new to me, though there was something in the tone of it that told me the bird was related to the wood-wagtail and to the water-wagtail or thrush. The strain was emphatic and quite loud, like the canary's, but very brief. The bird kept itself well secreted in the upper branches of the trees, and for a long time eluded my eye. I passed to and fro several times, and it seemed to break out afresh as I approached a certain little bend in the creek, and to cease after I had got beyond it; no doubt its nest was some-where in the vicinity. After some delay the bird was sighted and brought down. It proved to be the small, or northern, water-thrush (called also the New York water-thrush),—a new bird to me. In size it was noticeably smaller than the large, or Louisiana, water-thrush, as described by Audubon, but in other respects its general appearance was the same. It was a great treat to me, and again I felt myself in luck.

This bird was unknown to the older ornithologists, and is but poorly described by the new. It builds a mossy nest on the ground, or under the edge of a decayed log. A correspondent writes me that he has found it breeding on the mountains in Pennsylvania. The large-billed water-thrush is much the superior songster, but the present species has a very bright and cheerful strain. The specimen I saw, contrary to the habits of the family, kept in the treetops like a warbler, and seemed to be engaged in catching insects.

The birds were unusually plentiful and noisy about the head of this lake; robins, blue jays, and woodpeckers greeted me with their familiar notes. The blue jays found an owl or some wild animal a short distance above me, and, as is their custom on such occasions, proclaimed it at the top of their voices, and kept on till the darkness began to gather in the woods.

I also heard here, as I had at two or three other points in the course of the day, the peculiar, resonant hammering of some species of woodpecker upon the hard, dry limbs. It was unlike any sound of the kind I had ever before heard, and, repeated at intervals through the silent woods, was a very marked and characteristic feature. Its peculiarity was the ordered succession of the raps, which gave it the character of a premeditated performance. There were first three strokes following each other rapidly, then two much louder ones with longer intervals between them. I heard the drumming here, and the next day at sunset at Furlow Lake, the source of Dry Brook, and in no instance was the order varied. There was melody in it, such as a woodpecker knows how to evoke from a smooth dry branch. It suggested something quite as pleasing as the liveliest bird-song, and was if anything more woodsy and wild. As the yellow-bellied woodpecker was the most abundant species in these woods, I attributed it to him. It is the one sound that still links itself with those scenes in my mind.

At sunset the grouse began to drum in all parts of the woods about the lake. I could hear five at one time, *thump, thump, thump, thump, thr-r-r-r-r-rr*. It was a homely, welcome sound. As I returned to camp at twilight, along the shore of the lake, the frogs also were in full chorus. The older ones ripped out their responses to each other with terrific force and volume. I know of no other animal capable of giving forth so much sound, in proportion to its size, as a frog. Some of these seemed to bellow as loud as a two-year-old bull. They were of immense size, and very abundant. No frog-eater had ever been there. Near the shore we felled a tree which reached far out in the lake. Upon the trunk and branches the frogs had soon collected in large numbers, and gamboled and splashed about the half-submerged top, like a parcel of schoolboys, making nearly as much noise.

After dark, as I was frying the fish, a panful of the largest trout was accidentally capsized in the fire. With rueful countenances we contemplated the irreparable loss our commissariat had sustained by this mishap; but remembering there was virtue in ashes, we poked the half-consumed fish from the bed of coals and ate them, and they were good.

We lodged that night on a brush-heap and slept soundly. The green, yielding beech-twigs, covered with a buffalo robe, were equal to a hair mattress. The heat and smoke from a large fire kindled in the afternoon had banished every "no-see-em" from the locality, and in the morning the sun was above the mountain before we awoke.

I immediately started again for the inlet, and went far up

the stream toward its source. A fair string of trout for breakfast was my reward. The cattle with the bell were at the head of the valley, where they had passed the night. Most of them were two-year-old steers. They came up to me and begged for salt, and scared the fish by their importunities.

We finished our bread that morning, and ate every fish we could catch, and about ten o'clock prepared to leave the lake. The weather had been admirable, and the lake was a gem, and I would gladly have spent a week in the neighborhood; but the question of supplies was a serious one, and would brook no delay.

When we reached, on our return, the point where we had crossed the line of marked trees the day before, the question arose whether we should still trust ourselves to this line, or follow our own trail back to the spring and the battlement of rocks on the top of the mountain, and thence to the rock where the guide had left us. We decided in favor of the former course. After a march of three quarters of an hour the blazed trees ceased, and we concluded we were near the point at which we had parted with the guide. So we built a fire, laid down our loads, and cast about on all sides for some clew as to our exact locality. Nearly an hour was consumed in this manner and without any result. I came upon a brood of young grouse, which diverted me for a moment. The old one blustered about at a furious rate, trying to draw all attention to herself, while the young ones, which were unable to fly, hid themselves. She whined like a dog in great distress, and dragged herself along apparently with the greatest difficulty. As I pursued her, she ran very nimbly, and presently flew a few yards. Then, as I went on, she flew farther and farther each time, till at last she got up, and went humming through the woods as if she had no interest in them. I went back and caught one of the young, which had simply squatted close to the leaves. I took it up and set it on the palm of my hand, which it hugged as closely as if still upon the ground. I then put it in my coatsleeve, when it ran and nestled in my armpit.

When we met at the sign of the smoke, opinions differed as to the most feasible course. There was no doubt but that we could get out of the woods; but we wished to get out speedily, and as near as possible to the point where we had entered. Half ashamed of our timidity and indecision, we finally tramped away back to where we had crossed the line of blazed trees, followed our old trail to the spring on the top of the range, and, after much searching and scouring to the right and left, found ourselves at the very place we had left two hours before. Another deliberation and a divided council. But something must be done. It was then mid-afternoon, and the prospect of spending another night on the mountains, without food or drink, was not pleasant. So we moved down the ridge. Here another line of marked trees was found, the course of which formed an obtuse angle with the one we had followed. It kept on the top of the ridge for perhaps a mile, when it entirely disappeared, and we were as much adrift as ever. Then one of the party swore an oath, and said he was going out of those woods, hit or miss, and, wheeling to the right, instantly plunged over the brink of the mountain. The rest followed, but would fain have paused and ciphered away at their own uncertainties, to see if a certainty could not be arrived at as to where we would come out. But our bold leader was solving the problem in the right way. Down and down and still down we went, as if we were to bring up in the bowels of the earth. It was by far the steepest descent we had made, and we felt a grim satisfaction in knowing that we could not retrace our steps this time, be the issue what it might. As we paused on the brink of a ledge of rocks, we chanced to see through the trees distant cleared land. A house or barn also was dimly descried. This was encouraging; but we could not make out whether it was on Beaver Kill or Mill Brook or Dry Brook, and did not long stop to consider where it was. We at last brought up at the bottom of a deep gorge, through which flowed a rapid creek that literally swarmed with trout. But we were in no mood to catch them, and pushed on along the channel of the stream, sometimes leaping from rock to rock, and sometimes splashing heedlessly through the water, and speculating the while as to where we should probably come out. On the Beaver Kill, my companions thought; but, from the position of the sun, I said, on the Mill Brook, about six miles below our team; for I remembered having seen, in coming up this stream, a deep, wild valley that led up into the mountains, like this one. Soon the banks of the stream became lower, and we moved into the woods. Here we entered upon an obscure wood-road, which presently conducted us into the midst of a vast hemlock forest. The land had a gentle slope, and we wondered why the lumbermen and barkmen who prowl through these woods had left this fine tract untouched. Beyond this the forest was mostly birch and maple.

We were now close to the settlement, and began to hear human sounds. One rod more, and we were out of the woods. It took us a moment to comprehend the scene. Things looked very strange at first; but quickly they began to change and to put on familiar features. Some magic scene-shifting seemed to take place before my eyes, till, instead of the unknown settlement which I at first seemed to look upon, there stood the farmhouse at which we had stopped two days before, and at the same moment we heard the stamping of our team in the barn. We sat down and laughed heartily over our good luck. Our desperate venture had resulted better than we had dared to hope, and had shamed our wisest plans. At the house our arrival had been anticipated about this time, and dinner was being put upon the table.

It was then five o'clock, so that we had been in the woods just forty-eight hours; but if time is only phenomenal, as the philosophers say, and life only in feeling, as the poets aver, we were some months, if not years, older at that moment than we had been two days before. Yet younger, too,—though this be a paradox,—for the birches had infused into us some of their own suppleness and strength.

APRIL

If we represent the winter of our northern climate by a rugged snow-clad mountain, and summer by a broad fertile plain, then the intermediate belt, the hilly and breezy uplands, will stand for spring, with March reaching well up into the region of the snows, and April lapping well down upon the greening fields and unloosened currents, not beyond the limits of winter's sallying storms, but well within the vernal zone,—within the reach of the warm breath and subtle, quickening influences of the plain below. At its best, April is the tenderest of tender salads made crisp by ice or snow water. Its type is the first spear of grass. The senses—sight, hearing, smell—are as hungry for its delicate and almost spiritual tokens as the cattle are for the first bite of its fields. How it touches one and makes him both glad and sad! The voices of the arriving birds, the migrating fowls, the clouds of pigeons sweeping across the sky or filling the woods, the elfin horn of the first honey-bee venturing abroad in the middle of the day, the clear piping of the little frogs in the marshes at sundown, the campfire in the sugar-bush, the smoke seen afar rising over the trees, the tinge of green that comes so suddenly on the sunny knolls and slopes, the full translucent streams, the waxing and warming sun,—how these things and others like them are noted by the eager eye and ear! April is my natal month, and I am born again into new delight and new surprises at each return of it. Its name has an indescribable charm to me. Its two syllables are like the calls of the first birds,—like that of the phœbe-bird, or of the meadowlark. Its very snows are fertilizing, and are called the poor man's manure.

Then its odors! I am thrilled by its fresh and indescribable odors,—the perfume of the bursting sod, of the quickened roots and rootlets, of the mould under the leaves, of the fresh furrows. No other month has odors like it. The west wind the other day came fraught with a perfume that was to the sense of smell what a wild and delicate strain of music is to the ear. It was almost transcendental. I walked across the hill with my nose in the air taking it in. It lasted for two days. I imagined it came from the willows of a distant swamp, whose catkins were affording the bees their first pollen; or did it come from much farther,—from beyond the horizon, the accumulated breath of innumerable farms and budding forests? The main characteristic of these April odors is their uncloying freshness. They are not sweet, they are oftener bitter, they are penetrating and lyrical. I know well the odors of May and June, of the world of meadows and orchards bursting into bloom, but they are not so ineffable and immaterial and so stimulating to the sense as the incense of April.

The season of which I speak does not correspond with the April of the almanac in all sections of our vast geography. It answers to March in Virginia and Maryland, while in parts of New York and New England it laps well over into May. It begins when the partridge drums, when the hyla pipes, when the shad start up the rivers, when the grass greens in the spring runs, and it ends when the leaves are unfolding and the last snowflake dissolves in midair. It may be the first of May before the first swallow appears, before the whip-poor-will is heard, before the wood thrush sings; but it is April as long as there is snow upon the mountains, no matter what the almanac may say. Our April is, in fact, a kind of Alpine summer, full of such contrasts and touches of wild, delicate beauty as no other season affords. The deluded citizen fancies there is nothing enjoyable in the country till June, and so misses the freshest, tenderest part. It is as if one should miss strawberries and begin his fruit-eating with melons and peaches. These last are good,—supremely so, they are melting and luscious,—but nothing so thrills and penetrates the taste, and wakes up and teases the papillæ of the tongue, as the uncloying strawberry. What midsummer sweetness half so distracting as its brisk sub-acid flavor, and what splendor of full-leaved June can stir the blood like the best of leafless April?

One characteristic April feature, and one that delights me very much, is the perfect emerald of the spring runs while the fields are yet brown and sere,—strips and patches of the most vivid velvet green on the slopes and in the valleys. How the eye grazes there, and is filled and refreshed! I had forgotten what a marked feature this was until I recently rode in an open wagon for three days through a mountainous, pastoral country, remarkable for its fine springs. Those delicious green patches are yet in my eye. The fountains flowed with May. Where no springs occurred, there were hints and suggestions of springs about the fields and by the roadside in the freshened grass,— sometimes overflowing a space in the form of an actual fountain.

The water did not quite get to the surface in such places, but sent its influence.

The fields of wheat and rye, too, how they stand out of the April landscape,—great green squares on a field of brown or gray!

Among April sounds there is none more welcome or suggestive to me than the voice of the little frogs piping in the marshes. No bird-note can surpass it as a spring token; and as it is not mentioned, to my knowledge, by the poets and writers of other lands, I am ready to believe it is characteristic of our season alone. You may be sure April has really come when this little amphibian creeps out of the mud and inflates its throat. We talk of the bird inflating its throat, but you should see this tiny minstrel inflate *its* throat, which becomes like a large bubble, and suggests a drummer-boy with his drum slung very high. In this drum, or by the aid of it, the sound is produced. Generally the note is very feeble at first, as if the frost was not yet all out of the creature's throat, and only one voice will be heard, some prophet bolder than all the rest, or upon whom the quickening ray of spring has first fallen. And it often happens that he is stoned for his pains by the yet unpacified element, and is compelled literally to "shut up" beneath a fall of snow or a heavy frost. Soon, however, he lifts up his voice again with more confidence, and is joined by others and still others, till in due time, say toward the last of the month, there is a shrill musical uproar, as the sun is setting, in every marsh and bog in the land. It is a plaintive sound, and I have heard people from the city speak of it as lonesome and depressing, but to the lover of the country it is a pure spring melody. The little piper will sometimes climb a bulrush, to which he clings like a sailor to a mast, and send forth his shrill call. There is a Southern species, heard when you have reached the Potomac, whose note is far more harsh and crackling. To stand on the verge of a swamp vocal with these, pains and stuns the ear. The call of the Northern species is far more tender and musical.*

Then is there anything like a perfect April morning? One hardly knows what the sentiment of it is, but it is something very delicious. It is youth and hope. It is a new earth and a new sky. How the air transmits sounds, and what an awakening, prophetic character all sounds have! The distant barking of a dog, or the lowing of a cow, or the crowing of a cock, seems from out the heart of Nature, and to be a call to come forth. The great sun appears to have been reburnished, and there is something in his first glance above the eastern hills, and the way his eye-beams dart right and left and smite the rugged mountains into gold, that quickens the pulse and inspires the heart.

Across the fields in the early morning I hear some of the rare April birds,—the chewink and the brown thrasher. The robin, bluebird, song sparrow, phœbe-bird, etc., come in March; but these two ground-birds are seldom heard till toward the last of April. The ground-birds are all tree-singers or air-singers; they must have an elevated stage to speak from. Our long-tailed thrush, or thrasher, like its congeners the catbird and mockingbird, delights in a high branch of some solitary tree, whence it will pour out its rich and intricate warble for an hour together. This bird is the great American chipper. There is no other bird that I know of that can chip with such emphasis and military decision as this yellow-eyed songster.

* The Southern species is called the green hyla. I have since heard them in my neighborhood on the Hudson.

It is like the click of a giant gun-lock. Why is the thrasher so stealthy? It always seems to be going about on tiptoe. I never knew it to steal anything, and yet it skulks and hides like a fugitive from justice. One never sees it flying aloft in the air and traversing the world openly, like most birds, but it darts along fences and through bushes as if pursued by a guilty conscience. Only when the musical fit is upon it does it come up into full view, and invite the world to hear and behold.

The chewink is a shy bird also, but not stealthy. It is very inquisitive, and sets up a great scratching among the leaves, apparently to attract your attention. The male is perhaps the most conspicuously marked of all the ground-birds except the bobolink, being black above, bay on the sides, and white beneath. The bay is in compliment to the leaves he is forever scratching among,—they have rustled against his breast and sides so long that these parts have taken their color; but whence come the white and black? The bird seems to be aware that his color betrays him, for there are few birds in the woods so careful about keeping themselves screened from view. When in song, its favorite perch is the top of some high bush near to cover. On being disturbed at such times, it pitches down into the brush and is instantly lost to view.

This is the bird that Thomas Jefferson wrote to Wilson about, greatly exciting the latter's curiosity. Wilson was just then upon the threshold of his career as an ornithologist, and had made a drawing of the Canada jay which he sent to the President. It was a new bird, and in reply Jefferson called his attention to a "curious bird" which was everywhere to be heard, but scarcely ever to be seen. He had for twenty years interested the young sportsmen of his neighborhood to shoot one for him, but without success. "It is in all the forests, from spring to fall," he says in his letter, "and never but on the tops of the tallest trees, from which it perpetually serenades us with some of the sweetest notes, and as clear as those of the nightingale. I have followed it for miles, without ever but once getting a good view of it. It is of the size and make of the mockingbird, lightly thrush-colored on the back, and a grayish white on the breast and belly. Mr. Randolph, my son-in-law, was in possession of one which had been shot by a neighbor," etc. Randolph pronounced it a flycatcher, which was a good way wide of the mark. Jefferson must have seen only the female, after all his tramp, from his description of the color; but he was doubtless following his own great thoughts more than the bird, else he would have had an earlier view. The bird was not a new one, but was well known then as the ground-robin. The President put Wilson on the wrong scent by his erroneous description, and it was a long time before the latter got at the truth of the case. But Jefferson's letter is a good sample of those which specialists often receive from intelligent persons who have seen or heard something in their line very curious or entirely new, and who set the man of science agog by a description of the supposed novelty,—a description that generally fits the facts of the case about as well as your coat fits the chair-back. Strange and curious things in the air, and in the water, and in the earth beneath, are seen every day except by those who are looking for them, namely, the naturalists. When Wilson or Audubon gets his eye on the unknown bird, the illusion vanishes, and your phenomenon turns out to be one of the commonplaces of the fields or woods.

A prominent April bird, that one does not have to go to

the woods or away from his own door to see and hear, is the hardy and ever-welcome meadowlark. What a twang there is about this bird, and what vigor! It smacks of the soil. It is the winged embodiment of the spirit of our spring meadows. What emphasis in its "*z-d-t, z-d-t*," and what character in its long, piercing note! Its straight, tapering, sharp beak is typical of its voice. Its note goes like a shaft from a crossbow; it is a little too sharp and piercing when near at hand, but, heard in the proper perspective, it is eminently melodious and pleasing. It is one of the major notes of the fields at this season. In fact, it easily dominates all others. "*Spring o' the year! spring o' the year!*" it says, with a long-drawn breath, a little plaintive, but not complaining or melancholy. At times it indulges in something much more intricate and lark-like while hovering on the wing in midair, but a song is beyond the compass of its instrument, and the attempt usually ends in a breakdown. A clear, sweet, strong, high-keyed note, uttered from some knoll or rock, or stake in the fence, is its proper vocal performance. It has the build and walk and flight of the quail and the grouse. It gets up before you in much the same manner, and falls an easy prey to the crack shot. Its yellow breast, surmounted by a black crescent, it need not be ashamed to turn to the morning sun, while its coat of mottled gray is in perfect keeping with the stubble amid which it walks.

The two lateral white quills in its tail seem strictly in character. These quills spring from a dash of scorn and defiance in the bird's make-up. By the aid of these, it can almost emit a flash as it struts about the fields and jerks out its sharp notes. They give a rayed, a definite and piquant expression to its movements. This bird is not properly a lark, but a starling, say the ornithologists, though it is lark-like in its habits, being a walker and entirely a ground-bird. Its color also allies it to the true lark. I believe there is no bird in the English or European fields that answers to this hardy pedestrian of our meadows. He is a true American, and his note one of our characteristic April sounds.

Another marked April note, proceeding sometimes from the meadows, but more frequently from the rough pastures and borders of the woods, is the call of the high-hole, or golden-shafted woodpecker. It is quite as strong as that of the meadowlark, but not so long-drawn and piercing. It is a succession of short notes rapidly uttered, as if the bird said "*if-if-if-if-if-if-if*." The notes of the ordinary downy and hairy woodpeckers suggest, in some way, the sound of a steel punch; but that of the high-hole is much softer, and strikes on the ear with real springtime melody. The high-hole is not so much a woodpecker as he is a ground-pecker. He subsists largely on ants and crickets, and does not appear till they are to be found.

In Solomon's description of spring, the voice of the turtle is prominent, but our turtle, or mourning dove, though it arrives in April, can hardly be said to contribute noticeably to the open-air sounds. Its call is so vague, and soft, and mournful,—in fact, so remote and diffused,—that few persons ever hear it at all.

Such songsters as the cow blackbird are noticeable at this season, though they take a back seat a little later. It utters a peculiarly liquid April sound. Indeed, one would think its crop was full of water, its notes so bubble up and regurgitate, and are delivered with such an apparent stomachic contraction. This bird is the only feathered polygamist we have. The females are greatly in excess of the males, and the latter are usually attended by three or four of the former. As soon as the other birds begin to build, they are on the *qui vive*, prowling about like gypsies, not to steal the young of others, but to steal their eggs into other birds' nests, and so shirk the labor and responsibility of hatching and rearing their own young. As these birds do not mate, and as therefore there can be little or no rivalry or competition between the males, one wonders—in view of Darwin's teaching—why one sex should have brighter and richer plumage than the other, which is the fact. The males are easily distinguished from the dull and faded females by their deep glossy-black coats.

The April of English literature corresponds nearly to our May. In Great Britain, the swallow and the cuckoo usually arrive by the middle of April; with us, their appearance is a week or two later. Our April, at its best, is a bright, laughing face under a hood of snow, like the English March, but presenting sharper contrasts, a greater mixture of smiles and tears and icy looks than are known to our ancestral climate. Indeed, Winter sometimes retraces his steps in this month, and unburdens himself of the snows that the previous cold has kept back; but we are always sure of a number of radiant, equable days,—days that go before the bud, when the sun embraces the earth with fervor and determination. How his beams pour into the woods till the mould under the leaves is warm and emits an odor! The waters glint and sparkle, the birds gather in groups, and even those unwont to sing find a voice. On the streets of the cities, what a flutter, what bright looks and gay colors! I recall one preëminent day of this kind last April. I made a note of it in my note-book. The earth seemed suddenly to emerge from a wilderness of clouds and chilliness into one of these blue sunlit spaces. How the voyagers rejoiced! Invalids came forth, old men sauntered down the street, stocks went up, and the political outlook brightened.

Such days bring out the last of the hibernating animals. The woodchuck unrolls and creeps out of his den to see if his clover has started yet. The torpidity leaves the snakes and the turtles, and they come forth and bask in the sun. There is nothing so small, nothing so great, that it does not respond to these celestial spring days, and give the pendulum of life a fresh start.

April is also the month of the new furrow. As soon as the frost is gone and the ground settled, the plow is started upon the hill, and at each bout I see its brightened mould-board flash in the sun. Where the last remnants of the snowdrift lingered yesterday the plow breaks the sod to-day. Where the drift was deepest the grass is pressed flat, and there is a deposit of sand and earth blown from the fields to windward. Line upon line the turf is reversed, until there stands out of the neutral landscape a ruddy square visible for miles, or until the breasts of the broad hills glow like the breasts of the robins.

Then who would not have a garden in April? to rake together the rubbish and burn it up, to turn over the renewed soil, to scatter the rich compost, to plant the first seed, or bury the first tuber! It is not the seed that is planted, any more than it is I that is planted; it is not the dry stalks and weeds that are burned up, any more than it is my gloom and regrets that are consumed. An April smoke makes a clean harvest.

I think April is the best month to be born in. One is just in time, so to speak, to catch the first train, which is made up in this month. My April chickens always turn out best. They get an early start; they have rugged constitutions. Late chickens cannot stand the heavy dews, or withstand the predaceous hawks. In April all nature starts with you. You have not come out your hibernaculum too early or too late; the time is ripe, and, if you do not keep pace with the rest, why, the fault is not in the season.

A SUMMER VOYAGE

When one summer day I bethought me of a voyage down the east or Pepacton branch of the Delaware, I seemed to want some excuse for the start, some send-off, some preparation, to give the enterprise genesis and head. This I found in building my own boat. It was a happy thought. How else should I have got under way, how else should I have raised the breeze? The boat-building warmed the blood; it made the germ take; it whetted my appetite for the voyage. There is nothing like serving an apprenticeship to fortune, like earning the right to your tools. In most enterprises the temptation is always to begin too far along; we want to start where somebody else leaves off. Go back to the stump, and see what an impetus you get. Those fishermen who wind their own flies before they go a-fishing,—how they bring in the trout; and those hunters who run their own bullets or make their own cartridges,—the game is already mortgaged to them.

When my boat was finished—and it was a very simple affair—I was eager as a boy to be off; I feared the river would all run by before I could wet her bottom in it. This enthusiasm

begat great expectations of the trip. I should surely surprise
Nature and win some new secrets from her. I should glide down
noiselessly upon her and see what all those willow screens and
baffling curves concealed. As a fisherman and pedestrian I
had been able to come at the stream only at certain points:
now the most private and secluded retreats of the nymph would
be opened to me; every bend and eddy, every cove hedged in
by swamps or passage walled in by high alders, would be at
the beck of my paddle.

Whom shall one take with him when he goes a-courting
Nature? This is always a vital question. There are persons who
will stand between you and that which you seek: they obtrude
themselves; they monopolize your attention; they blunt your
sense of the shy, half-revealed intelligences about you. I want
for companion a dog or a boy, or a person who has the virtues
of dogs and boys,—transparency, good-nature, curiosity, open
sense, and a nameless quality that is akin to trees and growths
and the inarticulate forces of nature. With him you are alone,
and yet have company; you are free; you feel no disturbing
element; the influences of nature stream through him and
around him; he is a good conductor of the subtle fluid. The
quality or qualification I refer to belongs to most persons who
spend their lives in the open air,—to soldiers, hunters, fishers,
laborers, and to artists and poets of the right sort. How full of
it, to choose an illustrious example, was such a man as Walter
Scott!

But no such person came in answer to my prayer, so I set
out alone.

It was fit that I put my boat into the water at Arkville, but
it may seem a little incongruous that I should launch her into
Dry Brook; yet Dry Brook is here a fine large trout stream,

and I soon found its waters were wet enough for all practical purposes. The Delaware is only one mile distant, and I chose this as the easiest road from the station to it. A young farmer helped me carry the boat to the water, but did not stay to see me off; only some calves feeding alongshore witnessed my embarkation. It would have been a godsend to boys, but there were no boys about. I stuck on a rift before I had gone ten yards, and saw with misgiving the paint transferred from the bottom of my little scow to the tops of the stones thus early in the journey. But I was soon making fair headway, and taking trout for my dinner as I floated along. My first mishap was when I broke the second joint of my rod on a bass, and the first serious impediment to my progress was when I encountered the trunk of a prostrate elm bridging the stream within a few inches of the surface. My rod mended and the elm cleared, I anticipated better sailing when I should reach the Delaware itself; but I found on this day and on subsequent days that the Delaware has a way of dividing up that is very embarrassing to the navigator. It is a stream of many minds: its waters cannot long agree to go all in the same channel, and whichever branch I took I was pretty sure to wish I had taken one of the others. I was constantly sticking on rifts, where I would have to dismount, or running full tilt into willow banks, where I would lose my hat or endanger my fishing-tackle. On the whole, the result of my first day's voyaging was not encouraging. I made barely eight miles, and my ardor was a good deal dampened, to say nothing about my clothing. In mid-afternoon I went to a well-to-do-looking farmhouse and got some milk, which I am certain the thrifty housewife skimmed, for its blueness infected my spirits, and I went into camp that night more than half persuaded to abandon the enterprise in the morning. The loneliness of the river, too, unlike that of the fields and woods, to which I was more accustomed, oppressed me. In the woods, things are close to you, and you touch them and seem to interchange something with them; but upon the river, even though it be a narrow and shallow one like this, you are more isolated, farther removed from the soil and its attractions, and an easier prey to the unsocial demons. The long, unpeopled vistas ahead; the still, dark eddies; the endless monotone and soliloquy of the stream; the unheeding rocks basking like monsters along the shore, half out of the water, half in; a solitary heron starting up here and there, as you rounded some point, and flapping disconsolately ahead till lost to view, or standing like a gaunt spectre on the umbrageous side of the mountain, his motionless form revealed against the dark green as you passed; the trees and willows and alders that hemmed you in on either side, and hid the fields and the farmhouses and the road that ran near by,—these things and others aided the skimmed milk to cast a gloom over my spirits that argued ill for the success of my undertaking. Those rubber boots, too, that parboiled my feet and were clogs of lead about them,— whose spirits are elastic enough to endure them? A malediction upon the head of him who invented them! Take your old shoes, that will let the water in and let it out again, rather than stand knee-deep all day in these extinguishers.

I escaped from the river, that first night, and took to the woods, and profited by the change. In the woods I was at home again, and the bed of hemlock boughs salved my spirits. A cold spring run came down off the mountain, and beside it, underneath birches and hemlocks, I improvised my hearth-stone. In sleeping on the ground it is a great advantage to have a back-log; it braces and supports you, and it is a bedfellow that will not grumble when, in the middle of the night, you crowd sharply up against it. It serves to keep in the warmth, also. A heavy stone or other *point de résistance* at your feet is also a help. Or, better still, scoop out a little place in the earth, a few inches deep, so as to admit your body from your hips to your shoulders; you thus get an equal bearing the whole length of you. I am told the Western hunters and guides do this. On the same principle, the sand makes a good bed, and the snow. You make a mould in which you fit nicely. My berth that night was between two logs that the barkpeelers had stripped ten or more years before. As they had left the bark there, and as hemlock bark makes excellent fuel, I had more reasons than one to be grateful to them.

In the morning I felt much refreshed, and as if the night had tided me over the bar that threatened to stay my progress. If I can steer clear of skimmed milk, I said, I shall now finish the voyage of fifty miles to Hancock with increasing pleasure.

When one breaks camp in the morning, he turns back again and again to see what he has left. Surely, he feels, he has forgotten something; what is it? But it is only his own sad thoughts and musings he has left, the fragment of his life he has lived there. Where he hung his coat on the tree, where he slept on the boughs, where he made his coffee or broiled his trout over the coals, where he drank again and again at the little brown pool in the spring run, where he looked long and long up into the whispering branches overhead, he has left what he cannot bring away with him,—the flame and the ashes of himself.

Of certain game-birds it is thought that at times they have the power of withholding their scent; no hint or particle of themselves goes out upon the air. I think there are persons whose spiritual pores are always sealed up, and I presume they have the best time of it. Their hearts never radiate into the void; they do not yearn and sympathize without return; they do not leave themselves by the wayside as the sheep leaves her wool upon the brambles and thorns.

This branch of the Delaware, so far as I could learn, had never before been descended by a white man in a boat. Rafts of pine and hemlock timber are run down on the spring and fall freshets, but of pleasure-seekers in boats I appeared to be the first. Hence my advent was a surprise to most creatures in the water and out. I surprised the cattle in the field, and those ruminating leg-deep in the water turned their heads at my approach, swallowed their unfinished cuds, and scampered off as if they had seen a spectre. I surprised the fish on their spawning beds and feeding grounds; they scattered, as my shadow glided down upon them, like chickens when a hawk appears. I surprised an ancient fisherman seated on a spit of gravelly beach, with his back up stream, and leisurely angling in a deep, still eddy, and mumbling to himself. As I slid into the circle of his vision his grip on his pole relaxed, his jaw dropped, and he was too bewildered to reply to my salutation for some moments. As I turned a bend in the river I looked back, and saw him hastening away with great precipitation. I presume he had angled there for forty years without having his privacy thus intruded upon. I surprised hawks and herons and kingfishers. I came suddenly upon muskrats, and raced with them down the rifts, they having no time to take to their holes. At one point, as I rounded an elbow in the stream, a black eagle sprang from the top of a dead tree, and flapped hurriedly away. A kingbird gave chase, and disappeared for some moments in the gulf between the great wings of the eagle, and I imagined him seated upon his back delivering his puny blows upon the royal bird. I interrupted two or three minks fishing and hunting alongshore. They would dart under the bank when they saw me, then presently thrust out their sharp, weasel-like noses, to see if the danger was imminent. At one point, in a little cove behind the willows, I surprised some schoolgirls, with skirts amazingly abbreviated, wading and playing in the water. And as much surprised as any, I am sure, was that hard-worked-looking housewife, when I came up from under the bank in front of her house, and with pail in hand appeared at her door and asked for milk, taking the precaution to intimate that I had no objection to the yellow scum that is supposed to rise on a fresh article of that kind.

"What kind of milk do you want?"

"The best you have. Give me two quarts of it," I replied.

"What do you want to do with it?" with an anxious tone, as if I might want to blow up something or burn her barns with it.

"Oh, drink it," I answered, as if I frequently put milk to that use.

"Well, I suppose I can get you some"; and she presently reappeared with swimming pail, with those little yellow flakes floating about upon it that one likes to see.

I passed several low dams the second day, but had no trouble. I dismounted and stood upon the apron, and the boat, with plenty of line, came over as lightly as a chip, and swung around in the eddy below like a steed that knows its master. In the afternoon, while slowly drifting down a long eddy, the moist southwest wind brought me the welcome odor of strawberries, and running ashore by a meadow, a short distance below, I was soon parting the daisies and filling my cup with the dead-ripe fruit. Berries, be they red, blue, or black, seem like a special providence to the camper-out; they are luxuries he has not counted on, and I prized these accordingly. Later in the day it threatened rain, and I drew up to shore under the shelter of some thick overhanging hemlocks, and proceeded to eat my berries and milk, glad of an excuse not to delay my lunch longer. While tarrying here I heard young voices up stream, and looking in that direction saw two boys coming down the rapids on rude floats. They were racing along at a lively pace, each with a pole in his hand, dexterously avoiding the rocks and the breakers, and schooling themselves thus early in the duties and perils of the raftsmen. As they saw me one observed to the other,—

"There is the man we saw go by when we were building our floats. If we had known he was coming so far, maybe we could have got him to give us a ride."

They drew near, guided their crafts to shore beside me, and tied up, their poles answering for hawsers. They proved to be Johnny and Denny Dwire, aged ten and twelve. They were friendly boys, and though not a bit bashful were not a bit impertinent. And Johnny, who did the most of the talking, had such a sweet, musical voice; it was like a bird's. It seems Denny had run away, a day or two before, to his uncle's, five miles above, and Johnny had been after him, and was bringing his prisoner home on a float; and it was hard to tell which was enjoying the fun most, the captor or the captured.

"Why did you run away?" said I to Denny.

"Oh, 'cause," replied he, with an air which said plainly, "The reasons are too numerous to mention."

"Boys, you know, will do so, sometimes," said Johnny,

and he smiled upon his brother in a way that made me think they had a very good understanding upon the subject.

They could both swim, yet their floats looked very perilous,—three pieces of old plank or slabs, with two cross-pieces and a fragment of a board for a rider, and made without nails or withes.

"In some places," said Johnny, "one plank was here and another off there, but we managed, somehow, to keep atop of them."

"Let's leave our floats here, and ride with him the rest of the way," said one to the other.

"All right; may we, mister?"

I assented, and we were soon afloat again. How they enjoyed the passage; how smooth it was; how the boat glided along; how quickly she felt the paddle! They admired her much; they praised my steersmanship; they praised my fish-pole and all my fixings down to my hateful rubber boots. When we stuck on the rifts, as we did several times, they leaped out quickly, with their bare feet and legs, and pushed us off.

"I think," said Johnny, "if you keep her straight and let her have her own way, she will find the deepest water. Don't you, Denny?"

"I think she will," replied Denny; and I found the boys were pretty nearly right.

I tried them on a point of natural history. I had observed, coming along, a great many dead eels lying on the bottom of the river, that I supposed had died from spear wounds. "No," said Johnny, "they are lamper-eels. They die as soon as they have built their nests and laid their eggs."

"Are you sure?"

"That's what they all say, and I know they are lampers."

So I fished one up out of the deep water with my paddle-blade and examined it; and sure enough it was a lamprey. There was the row of holes along its head, and its ugly suction mouth. I had noticed their nests, too, all along, where the water in the pools shallowed to a few feet and began to hurry toward the rifts: they were low mounds of small stones, as if a bushel or more of large pebbles had been dumped upon the river bottom; occasionally they were so near the surface as to make a big ripple. The eel attaches itself to the stones by its mouth, and thus moves them at will. An old fisherman told me that a strong man could not pull a large lamprey loose from a rock to which it had attached itself. It fastens to its prey in this way, and sucks the life out. A friend of mine says he once saw in the St. Lawrence a pike as long as his arm with a lamprey eel attached to him. The fish was nearly dead and was quite white, the eel had so sucked out his blood and substance. The fish, when seized, darts against rocks and stones, and tries in vain to rub the eel off, then succumbs to the sucker.

"The lampers do not all die," said Denny, "because they do not all spawn"; and I observed that the dead ones were all of one size and doubtless of the same age.

The lamprey is the octopus, the devil-fish, of these waters, and there is, perhaps, no tragedy enacted here that equals that of one of these vampires slowly sucking the life out of a bass or a trout.

My boys went to school part of the time. Did they have a good teacher?

"Good enough for me," said Johnny.

"Good enough for me," echoed Denny.

Just below Bark-a-boom—the name is worth keeping—

they left me. I was loath to part with them; their musical voices and their thorough good-fellowship had been very acceptable. With a little persuasion, I think they would have left their home and humble fortunes, and gone a-roving with me.

About four o'clock the warm, vapor-laden southwest wind brought forth the expected thunder-shower. I saw the storm rapidly developing behind the mountains in my front. Presently I came in sight of a long covered wooden bridge that spanned the river about a mile ahead, and I put my paddle into the water with all my force to reach this cover before the storm. It was neck and neck most of the way. The storm had the wind, and I had it—in my teeth. The bridge was at Shavertown, and it was by a close shave that I got under it before the rain was upon me. How it poured and rattled and whipped in around the abutment of the bridge to reach me! I looked out well satisfied upon the foaming water, upon the wet, unpainted houses and barns of the Shavertowners, and upon the trees,

"Caught and cuffed by the gale."

Another traveler—the spotted-winged nighthawk—was also roughly used by the storm. He faced it bravely, and beat and beat, but was unable to stem it, or even hold his own; gradually he drifted back, till he was lost to sight in the wet obscurity. The water in the river rose an inch while I waited, about three quarters of an hour. Only one man, I reckon, saw me in Shavertown, and he came and gossiped with me from the bank above when the storm had abated.

The second night I stopped at the sign of the elm-tree. The woods were too wet, and I concluded to make my boat my bed. A superb elm, on a smooth grassy plain a few feet from the water's edge, looked hospitable in the twilight, and I drew my boat up beneath it. I hung my clothes on the jagged edges of its rough bark, and went to bed with the moon, "in her third quarter," peeping under the branches upon me. I had been reading Stevenson's amusing "Travels with a Donkey," and the lines he pretends to quote from an old play kept running in my head:—

> "The bed was made, the room was fit,
> By punctual eve the stars were lit;
> The air was sweet, the water ran;
> No need was there for maid or man,
> When we put up, my ass and I,
> At God's green caravanserai."

But the stately elm played me a trick: it slyly and at long intervals let great drops of water down upon me, now with a sharp smack upon my rubber coat; then with a heavy thud upon the seat in the bow or stern of my boat; then plump into my upturned ear, or upon my uncovered arm, or with a ring into my tin cup, or with a splash into my coffee-pail that stood at my side full of water from a spring I had just passed. After two hours' trial I found dropping off to sleep, under such circumstances, was out of the question; so I sprang up, in no very amiable mood toward my host, and drew my boat clean from under the elm. I had refreshing slumber thenceforth, and the birds were astir in the morning long before I was.

There is one way, at least, in which the denuding the country of its forests has lessened the rainfall: in certain conditions of the atmosphere every tree is a great condenser of moisture, as I had just observed in the case of the old elm; little showers are generated in their branches, and in the aggregate the amount of water precipitated in this way is considerable. Of a foggy summer morning one may see little puddles of water standing on the stones beneath maple-trees, along the street; and in winter, when there is a sudden change from cold to warm, with fog, the water fairly runs down the trunks of the trees, and streams from their naked branches. The temperature of the tree is so much below that of the atmosphere in such cases that the condensation is very rapid. In lieu of these arboreal rains we have the dew upon the grass, but it is doubtful if the grass ever drips as does a tree.

The birds, I say, were astir in the morning before I was, and some of them were more wakeful through the night, unless they sing in their dreams. At this season one may hear at intervals numerous bird voices during the night. The whippoor-will was piping when I lay down, and I still heard one when I woke up after midnight. I heard the song sparrow and the kingbird also, like watchers calling the hour, and several times I heard the cuckoo. Indeed, I am convinced that our cuckoo is to a considerable extent a night bird, and that he moves about freely from tree to tree. His peculiar guttural note, now here, now there, may be heard almost any summer night, in any part of the country, and occasionally his better known cuckoo call. He is a great recluse by day, but seems to wander abroad freely by night.

The birds do indeed begin with the day. The farmer who is in the field at work while he can yet see stars catches their first matin hymns. In the longest June days the robin strikes up about half past three o'clock, and is quickly followed by the song sparrow, the oriole, the catbird, the wren, the wood thrush, and all the rest of the tuneful choir. Along the Potomac I have heard the Virginia cardinal whistle so loudly and persistently in the treetops above, that sleeping after four o'clock was out of the question. Just before the sun is up, there is a marked lull, during which, I imagine, the birds are at breakfast. While building their nest, it is very early in the morning that they put in their big strokes; the back of their day's work is broken before you have begun yours.

A lady once asked me if there was any individuality among the birds, or if those of the same kind were as near alike as two peas. I was obliged to answer that to the eye those of the same species *were* as near alike as two peas, but that in their songs there were often marks of originality. Caged or domesticated birds develop notes and traits of their own, and among the more familiar orchard and garden birds one may notice the same tendency. I observe a great variety of songs, and even qualities of voice, among the orioles and among the song sparrows. On this trip my ear was especially attracted to some striking and original sparrow songs. At one point I was half afraid I had let pass an opportunity to identify a new warbler, but finally concluded it was a song sparrow. On another occasion I used to hear day after day a sparrow that appeared to have some organic defect in its voice: part of its song was scarcely above a whisper, as if the bird was suffering from a very bad cold. I have heard a bobolink and a hermit thrush with similar defects of voice. I have heard a robin with a part of the whistle of the quail in his song. It was out of time and out of tune, but the robin seemed insensible of the incongruity, and sang as loudly and as joyously as any of his mates. A catbird will sometimes show a special genius for mimicry, and I have known one to suggest very plainly some notes of the bobolink.

There are numerous long covered bridges spanning the Delaware, and under some of these I saw the cliff swallow at home, the nests being fastened to the under sides of the timbers,—as it were, suspended from the ceiling instead of being planted upon the shelving or perpendicular side, as is usual with them. To have laid the foundation, indeed, to have sprung the vault downward and finished it successfully, must have required special engineering skill. I had never before seen or heard of these nests being so placed. But birds are quick to adjust their needs to the exigencies of any case. Not long before, I had seen in a deserted house, on the head of the Rondout, the chimney swallows entering the chamber through a stove-pipe hole in the roof, and gluing their nests to the sides of the rafters, like the barn swallows.

I was now, on the third day, well down in the wilds of Colchester, with a current that made between two and three miles an hour,—just a summer idler's pace. The atmosphere of the river had improved much since the first day,—was, indeed, without taint,—and the water was sweet and good. There were farmhouses at intervals of a mile or so; but the amount of tillable land in the river valley or on the adjacent mountains was very small. Occasionally there would be forty or fifty acres of flat, usually in grass or corn, with a thrifty looking farmhouse. One could see how surely the land made the house and its surrounding; good land bearing good buildings, and poor land poor.

In mid-forenoon I reached the long placid eddy at Downsville, and here again fell in with two boys. They were out paddling about in a boat when I drew near, and they evidently regarded me in the light of a rare prize which fortune had wafted them.

"Ain't you glad we come, Benny?" I heard one of them observe to the other, as they were conducting me to the best place to land. They were bright, good boys, off the same piece as my acquaintances of the day before, and about the same ages,—differing only in being village boys. With what curiosity they looked me over! Where had I come from; where was I going; how long had I been on the way; who built my boat; was I a carpenter, to build such a neat craft, etc.? They never had seen such a traveler before. Had I had no mishaps? And then they bethought them of the dangerous passes that awaited me, and in good faith began to warn and advise me. They had heard the tales of raftsmen, and had conceived a vivid idea of the perils of the river below, gauging their notions of it from the spring and fall freshets tossing about the heavy and cumbrous rafts. There was a whirlpool, a rock eddy, and a binocle within a mile. I might be caught in the binocle, or engulfed in the whirlpool, or smashed up in the eddy. But I felt much reassured when they told me I had already passed several whirlpools and rock eddies; but that terrible binocle,—what was that? I had never heard of such a monster. Oh, it was a still, miry place at the head of a big eddy. The current might carry me up there, but I could easily get out again; the rafts did. But there was another place I must beware of, where two eddies faced each other; raftsmen were sometimes swept off there by the oars and drowned. And when I came to rock eddy, which I would know, because the river divided there (a part of the water being afraid to risk the eddy, I suppose), I must go ashore and survey the pass; but in any case it would be prudent to keep to the left. I might stick on the rift, but that was nothing to being wrecked upon those rocks. The boys were quite in earnest, and I told them I would walk up to the village and post some letters to my friends before I braved all these dangers. So they marched me up the street, pointing out to their chums what they had found.

"Going way to Phil— What place is that near where the river goes into the sea?"

"Philadelphia?"

"Yes; thinks he may go way there. Won't he have fun?"

The boys escorted me about the town, then back to the river, and got in their boat and came down to the bend, where they could see me go through the whirlpool and pass the binocle (I am not sure about the orthography of the word, but I suppose it means a double, or a sort of mock eddy). I looked back as I shot over the rough current beside a gentle vortex, and saw them watching me with great interest. Rock eddy, also, was quite harmless, and I passed it without any preliminary survey.

I nooned at Sodom, and found good milk in a humble cottage. In the afternoon I was amused by a great blue heron that kept flying up in advance of me. Every mile or so, as I rounded some point, I would come unexpectedly upon him, till finally he grew disgusted with my silent pursuit, and took a long turn to the left up along the side of the mountain, and passed back up the river, uttering a hoarse, low note.

The wind still boded rain, and about four o'clock, announced by deep-toned thunder and portentous clouds, it began to charge down the mountain-side in front of me. I ran ashore, covered my traps, and took my way up through an orchard to a quaint little farmhouse. But there was not a soul about, outside or in, that I could find, though the door was unfastened; so I went into an open shed with the hens, and lounged upon some straw, while the unloosed floods came down. It was better than boating or fishing. Indeed, there are few summer pleasures to be placed before that of reclining at ease directly under a sloping roof, after toil or travel in the hot sun, and looking out into the rain-drenched air and fields. It is such a vital yet soothing spectacle. We sympathize with the earth. We know how good a bath is, and the unspeakable deliciousness of water to a parched tongue. The office of the sunshine is slow, subtle, occult, unsuspected; but when the clouds do their work the benefaction is so palpable and copious, so direct and whole-sale, that all creatures take note of it, and for the most part rejoice in it. It is a completion, a consummation, a paying of a debt with a royal hand; the measure is heaped and overflow-ing. It was the simple vapor of water that the clouds borrowed of the earth; now they pay back more than water: the drops are charged with electricity and with the gases of the air, and have new solvent powers. Then, how the slate is sponged off, and left all clean and new again!

In the shed where I was sheltered were many relics and odds and ends of the farm. In juxtaposition with two of the most stalwart wagon or truck-wheels I ever looked upon, was a cradle of ancient and peculiar make,—an aristocratic cradle, with high-turned posts and an elaborately carved and moulded body, that was suspended upon rods and swung from the top. How I should have liked to hear its history and the story of the lives it had rocked, as the rain sang and the boughs tossed without! Above it was the cradle of a phœbe-bird saddled upon a stick that ran behind the rafter; its occupants had not flown, and its story was easy to read.

Soon after the first shock of the storm was over, and before I could see breaking sky, the birds tuned up with new ardor,—the robin, the indigo bird, the purple finch, the song sparrow, and in the meadow below the bobolink. The cockerel

near me followed suit, and repeated his refrain till my meditations were so disturbed that I was compelled to eject him
from the cover, albeit he had the best right there. But he crowed
his defiance with drooping tail from the yard in front. I, too,
had mentally crowed over the good fortune of the shower; but
before I closed my eyes that night my crest was a good deal
fallen, and I could have wished the friendly elements had not
squared their accounts quite so readily and uproariously.

The one shower did not exhaust the supply a bit; Nature's
hand was full of trumps yet,—yea, and her sleeve too. I stopped
at a trout brook, which came down out of the mountains on
the right, and took a few trout for my supper; but its current
was too roily from the shower for fly-fishing. Another farmhouse
attracted me, but there was no one at home; so I picked a quart
of strawberries in the meadow in front, not minding the wet
grass, and about six o'clock, thinking another storm that had
been threatening on my right had miscarried, I pushed off,
and went floating down into the deepening gloom of the river
valley. The mountains, densely wooded from base to summit,
shut in the view on every hand. They cut in from the right and
from the left, one ahead of the other, matching like the teeth
of an enormous trap; the river was caught and bent, but not
long detained, by them. Presently I saw the rain creeping slowly
over them in my rear, for the wind had changed; but I appre-
hended nothing but a moderate sundown drizzle, such as we
often get from the tail end of a shower, and drew up in the
eddy of a big rock under an overhanging tree till it should have
passed. But it did not pass; it thickened and deepened, and
reached a steady pour by the time I had calculated the sun
would be gilding the mountain-tops. I had wrapped my rubber
coat about my blankets and groceries, and bared my back to

the storm. In sullen silence I saw the night settling down and the rain increasing; my roof-tree gave way, and every leaf poured its accumulated drops upon me. There were streams and splashes where before there had been little more than a mist. I was getting well soaked and uncomplimentary in my remarks on the weather. A saucy catbird, near by, flirted and squealed very plainly, "There! there! What did I tell you! what did I tell you! Pretty pickle! pretty pickle! pretty pickle to be in!" But I had been in worse pickles, though if the water had been salt my pickling had been pretty thorough. Seeing the wind was in the northeast, and that the weather had fairly stolen a march on me, I let go my hold of the tree, and paddled rapidly to the opposite shore, which was low and pebbly, drew my boat up on a little peninsula, turned her over upon a spot which I cleared of its coarser stone, propped up one end with the seat, and crept beneath. I would now test the virtues of my craft as a roof, and I found she was without flaw, though she was pretty narrow. The tension of her timber was such that the rain upon her bottom made a low, musical hum.

Crouched on my blankets and boughs,—for I had gathered a good supply of the latter before the rain overtook me,—and dry only about my middle, I placidly took life as it came. A great blue heron flew by, and let off something like ironical horse laughter. Before it became dark I proceeded to eat my supper,—my berries, but not my trout. What a fuss we make about the "hulls" upon strawberries! We are hypercritical; we may yet be glad to dine off the hulls alone. Some people see something to pick and carp at in every good that comes to them; I was thankful that I had the berries, and resolutely ignored their little scalloped ruffles, which I found pleased the eye and did not disturb the palate.

When bedtime arrived, I found undressing a little awkward, my berth was so low; there was plenty of room in the aisle, and the other passengers were nowhere to be seen, but I did not venture out. It rained nearly all night, but the train made good speed, and reached the land of daybreak nearly on time. The water in the river had crept up during the night to within a few inches of my boat, but I rolled over and took another nap, all the same. Then I arose, had a delicious bath in the sweet, swift-running current, and turned my thoughts toward breakfast. The making of the coffee was the only serious problem. With everything soaked and a fine rain still falling, how shall one build a fire? I made my way to a little island above in quest of driftwood. Before I had found the wood I chanced upon another patch of delicious wild strawberries, and took an appetizer of them out of hand. Presently I picked up a yellow birch stick the size of my arm. The wood was decayed, but the bark was perfect. I broke it in two, punched out the rotten wood, and had the bark intact. The fatty or resinous substance in this bark preserves it, and makes it excellent kindling. With some seasoned twigs and a scrap of paper I soon had a fire going that answered my every purpose. More berries were picked while the coffee was brewing, and the breakfast was a success.

The camper-out often finds himself in what seems a distressing predicament to people seated in their snug, well-ordered houses; but there is often a real satisfaction when things come to their worst,—a satisfaction in seeing what a small matter it is, after all; that one is really neither sugar nor salt, to be afraid of the wet; and that life is just as well worth living beneath a scow or a dug-out as beneath the highest and broadest roof in Christendom.

By ten o'clock it became necessary to move, on account of the rise of the water, and as the rain had abated I picked up and continued my journey. Before long, however, the rain increased again, and I took refuge in a barn. The snug, tree-embowered farmhouse looked very inviting, just across the road from the barn; but as no one was about, and no faces appeared at the window that I might judge of the inmates, I contented myself with the hospitality the barn offered, filling my pockets with some dry birch shavings I found there where the farmer had made an ox-yoke, against the needs of the next kindling.

After an hour's detention I was off again. I stopped at Baxter's Brook, which flows hard by the classic hamlet of Harvard, and tried for trout, but with poor success, as I did not think it worth while to go far up stream.

At several points I saw rafts of hemlock lumber tied to the shore, ready to take advantage of the first freshet. Rafting is an important industry for a hundred miles or more along the Delaware. The lumbermen sometimes take their families or friends, and have a jollification all the way to Trenton or to Philadelphia. In some places the speed is very great, almost equaling that of an express train. The passage of such places as Cochecton Falls and "Foul Rift" is attended with no little danger. The raft is guided by two immense oars, one before and one behind. I frequently saw these huge implements in the driftwood alongshore, suggesting some colossal race of men. The raftsmen have names of their own. From the upper Delaware, where I had set in, small rafts are run down which they call "colts." They come frisking down at a lively pace. At Hancock they usually couple two rafts together, when I suppose they have a span of colts; or do two colts make one horse? Some parts of the framework of the raft they call "grubs"; much depends upon these grubs. The lumbermen were and are a hardy, virile race. The Hon. Charles Knapp, of Deposit, now eighty-three years of age, but with the look and step of a man of sixty, told me he had stood nearly all one December day in the water to his waist, reconstructing his raft, which had gone to pieces on the head of an island. Mr. Knapp had passed the first half of his life in Colchester and Hancock, and, although no sportsman, had once taken part in a great bear hunt there. The bear was an enormous one, and was hard pressed by a gang of men and dogs. Their muskets and assaults upon the beast with clubs had made no impression. Mr. Knapp saw where the bear was coming, and he thought he would show them how easy it was to dispatch a bear with a club, if you only knew where to strike. He had seen how quickly the largest hog would wilt beneath a slight blow across the "small of the back." So, armed with an immense hand-spike, he took up a position by a large rock that the bear must pass. On she came, panting and nearly exhausted, and at the right moment down came the club with great force upon the small of her back. "If a fly had alighted upon her," said Mr. Knapp, "I think she would have paid just as much attention to it as she did to me."

Early in the afternoon I encountered another boy, Henry Ingersoll, who was so surprised by my sudden and unwonted appearance that he did not know east from west. "Which way is west?" I inquired, to see if my own head was straight on the subject.

"That way," he said, indicating east within a few degrees.

"You are wrong," I replied. "Where does the sun rise?"

"There," he said, pointing almost in the direction he had pointed before.

"But does not the sun rise in the east here as well as elsewhere?" I rejoined.

"Well, they call that west, anyhow."

But Henry's needle was subjected to a disturbing influence just then. His house was near the river, and he was its sole guardian and keeper for the time; his father had gone up to the next neighbor's (it was Sunday), and his sister had gone with the schoolmistress down the road to get black birch. He came out in the road, with wide eyes, to view me as I passed, when I drew rein, and demanded the points of the compass, as above. Then I shook my sooty pail at him and asked for milk. Yes, I could have some milk, but I would have to wait till his sister came back; after he had recovered a little, he concluded he could get it. He came for my pail, and then his boyish curiosity appeared. My story interested him immensely. He had seen twelve summers, but he had only been four miles from home up and down the river: he had been down to the East Branch, and he had been up to Trout Brook. He took a pecuniary interest in me. What did my pole cost? What my rubber coat, and what my revolver? The latter he must take in his hand; he had never seen such a thing to shoot with before in *his* life, etc. He thought I might make the trip cheaper and easier by stage and by the cars. He went to school: there were six scholars in summer, one or two more in winter. The population is not crowded in the town of Hancock, certainly, and never will be. The people live close to the bone, as Thoreau would say, or rather close to the stump. Many years ago the young men there resolved upon having a ball. They concluded not to go to a hotel, on account of the expense, and so chose a private house. There was a man in the neighborhood who could play the fife; he offered to furnish the music for seventy-five cents. But this was deemed too much, so one of the party agreed to whistle. History does not tell how many beaux there were bent upon this reckless enterprise, but there were three girls. For refreshments they bought a couple of gallons of whiskey and a few pounds of sugar. When the spree was over, and the expenses were reckoned up, there was a shilling—a York shilling—apiece to pay. Some of the revelers were dissatisfied with this charge, and intimated that the managers had not counted themselves in, but taxed the whole expense upon the rest of the party.

As I moved on I saw Henry's sister and the schoolmistress picking their way along the muddy road near the river's bank. One of them saw me, and, dropping her skirts, said to the other (I could read the motions), "See that man!" The other lowered her flounces, and looked up and down the road, then glanced over into the field, and lastly out upon the river. They paused and had a good look at me, though I could see that their impulse to run away, like that of a frightened deer, was strong.

At the East Branch the Big Beaver Kill joins the Delaware, almost doubling its volume. Here I struck the railroad, the forlorn Midland, and here another set of men and manners cropped out,—what may be called the railroad conglomerate overlying this mountain freestone.

"Where did you steal that boat?" and "What you running away for?" greeted me from a handcar that went by.

I paused for some time and watched the fish hawks, or ospreys, of which there were nearly a dozen sailing about above the junction of the two streams, squealing and diving, and occasionally striking a fish on the rifts. I am convinced that the fish hawk sometimes feeds on the wing. I saw him do it

on this and on another occasion. He raises himself by a peculiar
motion, and brings his head and his talons together, and apparently takes a bite of a fish. While doing this his flight
presents a sharply undulating line; at the crest of each rise the
morsel is taken.

In a long, deep eddy under the west shore I came upon a
brood of wild ducks, the hooded merganser. The young were
about half grown, but of course entirely destitute of plumage.
They started off at great speed, kicking the water into foam
behind them, the mother duck keeping upon their flank and
rear. Near the outlet of the pool I saw them go ashore, and I
expected they would conceal themselves in the woods; but as
I drew near the place they came out, and I saw by their motions
they were going to make a rush by me up stream. At a signal
from the old one, on they came, and passed within a few feet
of me. It was almost incredible, the speed they made. Their
pink feet were like swiftly revolving wheels placed a little to
the rear; their breasts just skimmed the surface, and the water
was beaten into spray behind them. They had no need of wings;
even the mother bird did not use hers; a steamboat could hardly
have kept up with them. I dropped my paddle and cheered.
They kept the race up for a long distance, and I saw them
making a fresh spirt as I entered upon the rift and dropped
quickly out of sight. I next disturbed an eagle in his meditations
upon a dead treetop, and a cat sprang out of some weeds near
the foot of the tree. Was he watching for puss, while she was
watching for some smaller prey?

I passed Partridge Island—which is or used to be the name
of a post-office—unwittingly, and encamped for the night on
an island near Hawk's Point. I slept in my boat on the beach,
and in the morning my locks were literally wet with the dews

of the night, and my blankets too; so I waited for the sun to dry them. As I was gathering driftwood for a fire, a voice came over from the shadows of the east shore: "Seems to me you lay abed pretty late!"

"I call this early," I rejoined, glancing at the sun.

"Wall, it may be airly in the forenoon, but it ain't very airly in the mornin' "; a distinction I was forced to admit. Before I had reëmbarked some cows came down to the shore, and I watched them ford the river to the island. They did it with great ease and precision. I was told they will sometimes, during high water, swim over to the islands, striking in well up stream, and swimming diagonally across. At one point some cattle had crossed the river, and evidently got into mischief, for a large dog rushed them down the bank into the current, and worried them all the way over, part of the time swimming and part of the time leaping very high, as a dog will in deep snow, coming down with a great splash. The cattle were shrouded with spray as they ran, and altogether it was a novel picture.

My voyage ended that forenoon at Hancock, and was crowned by a few idyllic days with some friends in their cottage in the woods by Lake Oquaga, a body of crystal water on the hills near Deposit, and a haven as peaceful and perfect as voyager ever came to port in.

AN IDYL OF THE
HONEY-BEE

There is no creature with which man has surrounded himself that seems so much like a product of civilization, so much like the result of development on special lines and in special fields, as the honey-bee. Indeed, a colony of bees, with their neatness and love of order, their division of labor, their public-spiritedness, their thrift, their complex economies, and their inordinate love of gain, seems as far removed from a condition of rude nature as does a walled city or a cathedral town. Our native bee, on the other hand, the "burly, dozing humblebee," affects one more like the rude, untutored savage. He has learned nothing from experience. He lives from hand to mouth. He luxuriates in time of plenty, and he starves in times of scarcity. He lives in a rude nest, or in a hole in the ground, and in small communities; he builds a few deep cells or sacks in which he stores a little honey and bee-bread for his young, but as a worker in wax he is of the most primitive and awkward. The Indian regarded the honey-bee as an ill-omen. She was the white man's fly. In fact she was the epitome of the white man himself. She has the white

man's craftiness, his industry, his architectural skill, his neatness and love of system, his foresight; and, above all, his
eager, miserly habits. The honey-bee's great ambition is to be
rich, to lay up great stores, to possess the sweet of every flower
that blooms. She is more than provident. Enough will not satisfy
her; she must have all she can get by hook or by crook. She
comes from the oldest country, Asia, and thrives best in the
most fertile and long-settled lands.

Yet the fact remains that the honey-bee is essentially a
wild creature, and never has been and cannot be thoroughly
domesticated. Its proper home is the woods, and thither every
new swarm counts on going; and thither many do go in spite
of the care and watchfulness of the bee-keeper. If the woods
in any given locality are deficient in trees with suitable cavities,
the bees resort to all sorts of makeshifts; they go into chimneys,
into barns and outhouses, under stones, into rocks, and so
forth. Several chimneys in my locality with disused flues are
taken possession of by colonies of bees nearly every season.
One day, while bee-hunting, I developed a line that went
toward a farmhouse where I had reason to believe no bees were
kept. I followed it up and questioned the farmer about his bees.
He said he kept no bees, but that a swarm had taken possession
of his chimney, and another had gone under the clapboards
in the gable end of his house. He had taken a large lot of
honey out of both places the year before. Another farmer told
me that one day his family had seen a number of bees examining
a knothole in the side of his house; the next day, as they were
sitting down to dinner, their attention was attracted by a loud
humming noise, when they discovered a swarm of bees settling
upon the side of the house and pouring into the knothole. In
subsequent years other swarms came to the same place.

Apparently every swarm of bees, before it leaves the parent hive, sends out exploring parties to look up the future home. The woods and groves are searched through and through, and no doubt the privacy of many a squirrel and many a wood-mouse is intruded upon. What cozy nooks and retreats they do spy out, so much more attractive than the painted hive in the garden, so much cooler in summer and so much warmer in winter!

The bee is in the main an honest citizen: she prefers legitimate to illegitimate business; she is never an outlaw until her proper sources of supply fail; she will not touch honey as long as honey yielding flowers can be found; she always prefers to go to the fountain-head, and dislikes to take her sweets at second hand. But in the fall, after the flowers have failed, she can be tempted. The bee-hunter takes advantage of this fact; he betrays her with a little honey. He wants to steal her stores, and he first encourages her to steal his, then follows the thief home with her booty. This is the whole trick of the bee-hunter. The bees never suspect his game, else by taking a circuitous route they could easily baffle him. But the honey-bee has absolutely no wit or cunning outside of her special gifts as a gatherer and storer of honey. She is a simple-minded creature, and can be imposed upon by any novice. Yet it is not every novice that can find a bee-tree. The sportsman may track his game to its retreat by the aid of his dog, but in hunting the honey-bee one must be his own dog, and track his game through an element in which it leaves no trail. It is a task for a sharp, quick eye, and may test the resources of the best woodcraft. One autumn, when I devoted much time to this pursuit, as the best means of getting at nature and the open-air exhilaration, my eye became so trained that bees were nearly as easy to it as birds. I saw and heard bees wherever I went. One day, standing on a street corner in a great city, I saw above the trucks and the traffic a line of bees carrying off sweets from some grocery or confectionery shop.

One looks upon the woods with a new interest when he suspects they hold a colony of bees. What a pleasing secret it is,—a tree with a heart of comb honey, a decayed oak or maple with a bit of Sicily or Mount Hymettus stowed away in its trunk or branches; secret chambers where lies hidden the wealth of ten thousand little freebooters, great nuggets and wedges of precious ore gathered with risk and labor from every field and wood about!

But if you would know the delights of bee-hunting, and how many sweets such a trip yields besides honey, come with me some bright, warm, late September or early October day. It is the golden season of the year, and any errand or pursuit that takes us abroad upon the hills or by the painted woods and along the amber-colored streams at such a time is enough. So, with haversacks filled with grapes and peaches and apples and a bottle of milk,—for we shall not be home to dinner,— and armed with a compass, a hatchet, a pail, and a box with a piece of comb honey neatly fitted into it,—any box the size of your hand with a lid will do nearly as well as the elaborate and ingenious contrivance of the regular bee-hunter,—we sally forth. Our course at first lies along the highway under great chestnut-trees whose nuts are just dropping, then through an orchard and across a little creek, thence gently rising through a long series of cultivated fields toward some high uplying land behind which rises a rugged wooded ridge or mountain, the most sightly point in all this section. Behind this ridge for several miles the country is wild, wooded, and rocky, and is no doubt the home of many wild swarms of bees. What a gleeful uproar the robins, cedar-birds, high-holes, and cow blackbirds make amid the black cherry trees as we pass along! The raccoons, too, have been here after black cherries, and we see their marks at various points. Several crows are walking about a newly sowed wheatfield we pass through, and we pause to note their graceful movements and glossy coats. I have seen no bird walk the ground with just the same air the crow does. It is not exactly pride; there is no strut or swagger in it, though perhaps just a little condescension; it is the contented, complaisant, and self-possessed gait of a lord over his domains. All these acres are mine, he says, and all these crops; men plow and sow for me, and I stay here or go there, and find life sweet and good wherever I am. The hawk looks awkward and out of place on the ground; the game-birds hurry and skulk; but the crow is at home, and treads the earth as if there were none to molest or make him afraid.

The crows we have always with us, but it is not every day or every season that one sees an eagle. Hence I must preserve the memory of one I saw the last day I went bee-hunting. As I was laboring up the side of a mountain at the head of a valley, the noble bird sprang from the top of a dry tree above me and came sailing directly over my head. I saw him bend his eye down upon me, and I could hear the low hum of his plumage as if the web of every quill in his great wings vibrated in his strong, level flight. I watched him as long as my eye could hold him. When he was fairly clear of the mountain he began that sweeping spiral movement in which he climbs the sky. Up and up he went, without once breaking his majestic poise, till he appeared to sight some far-off alien geography, when he bent his course thitherward and gradually vanished in the blue depths. The eagle is a bird of large ideas; he embraces long distances; the continent is his home. I never look upon one without emotion; I follow him with my eye as long as I can. I think of Canada, of the Great Lakes, of the Rocky Mountains, of the wild and sounding seacoast. The waters are his, and the woods and the inaccessible cliffs. He pierces behind the veil of the storm, and his joy is height and depth and vast spaces.

We go out of our way to touch at a spring run in the edge of the woods, and are lucky to find a single scarlet lobelia lingering there. It seems almost to light up the gloom with its intense bit of color. Beside a ditch in a field beyond, we find the great blue lobelia, and near it, amid the weeds and wild grasses and purple asters, the most beautiful of our fall flowers, the fringed gentian. What a rare and delicate, almost aristo-cratic look the gentian has amid its coarse, unkempt surround-ings! It does not lure the bee, but it lures and holds every passing human eye. If we strike through the corner of yonder woods, where the ground is moistened by hidden springs, and where there is a little opening amid the trees, we shall find the closed gentian, a rare flower in this locality. I had walked this way many times before I chanced upon its retreat, and then I was following a line of bees. I lost the bees, but I got the gentians. How curious this flower looks with its deep blue petals folded together so tightly,—a bud and yet a blossom. It is the nun among our wild flowers,—a form closely veiled and cloaked. The buccaneer bumblebee sometimes tries to rifle it of its sweets. I have seen the blossom with the bee entombed in it. He had forced his way into the virgin corolla as if de-termined to know its secret, but he had never returned with the knowledge he had gained.

After a refreshing walk of a couple of miles we reach a
point where we will make our first trial,—a high stone wall
that runs parallel with the wooded ridge referred to, and sep-
arated from it by a broad field. There are bees at work there
on that goldenrod, and it requires but little manœuvring to
sweep one into our box. Almost any other creature rudely and
suddenly arrested in its career, and clapped into a cage in this
way, would show great confusion and alarm. The bee is alarmed
for a moment, but the bee has a passion stronger than its love
of life or fear of death, namely, desire for honey, not simply
to eat, but to carry home as booty. "Such rage of honey in
their bosom beats," says Virgil. It is quick to catch the scent
of honey in the box, and as quick to fall to filling itself. We
now set the box down upon the wall and gently remove the
cover. The bee is head and shoulders in one of the half-filled
cells, and is oblivious to everything else about it. Come rack,
come ruin, it will die at work. We step back a few paces, and
sit down upon the ground so as to bring the box against the
blue sky as a background. In two or three minutes the bee is
seen rising slowly and heavily from the box. It seems loath to
leave so much honey behind, and it marks the place well. It
mounts aloft in a rapidly increasing spiral, surveying the near
and minute objects first, then the larger and more distant, till,
having circled above the spot five or six times and taken all
its bearings, it darts away for home. It is a good eye that holds
fast to the bee till it is fairly off. Sometimes one's head will
swim following it, and often one's eyes are put out by the sun.
This bee gradually drifts down the hill, then strikes away toward
a farmhouse half a mile away where I know bees are kept.
Then we try another and another, and the third bee, much to
our satisfaction, goes straight toward the woods. We could see

the brown speck against the darker background for many yards. The regular bee-hunter professes to be able to tell a wild bee from a tame one by the color, the former, he says, being lighter. But there is no difference; they are both alike in color and in manner. Young bees are lighter than old, and that is all there is of it. If a bee lived many years in the woods it would doubtless come to have some distinguishing marks, but the life of a bee is only a few months at the farthest, and no change is wrought in this brief time.

Our bees are all soon back, and more with them, for we have touched the box here and there with the cork of a bottle of anise oil, and this fragrant and pungent oil will attract bees half a mile or more. When no flowers can be found, this is the quickest way to obtain a bee.

It is a singular fact that when the bee first finds the hunter's box, its first feeling is one of anger; it is as mad as a hornet; its tone changes, it sounds its shrill war trumpet and darts to and fro, and gives vent to its rage and indignation in no uncertain manner. It seems to scent foul play at once. It says, "Here is robbery; here is the spoil of some hive, may be my own," and its blood is up. But its ruling passion soon comes to the surface, its avarice gets the better of its indignation, and it seems to say, "Well, I had better take possession of this and carry it home." So after many feints and approaches and dartings off with a loud angry hum as if it would none of it, the bee settles down and fills itself.

It does not entirely cool off and get soberly to work till it has made two or three trips home with its booty. When other bees come, even if all from the same swarm, they quarrel and dispute over the box, and clip and dart at each other like bantam cocks. Apparently the ill feeling which the sight of the honey awakens is not one of jealousy or rivalry, but wrath.

A bee will usually make three or four trips from the hunter's box before it brings back a companion. I suspect the bee does not tell its fellows what it has found, but that they smell out the secret; it doubtless bears some evidence with it upon its feet or proboscis that it has been upon honeycomb and not upon flowers, and its companions take the hint and follow, arriving always many seconds behind. Then the quantity and quality of the booty would also betray it. No doubt, also, there are plenty of gossips about a hive that note and tell everything. "Oh, did you see that? Peggy Mel came in a few moments ago in great haste, and one of the upstairs packers says she was loaded till she groaned with apple-blossom honey, which she deposited, and then rushed off again like mad. Apple-blossom honey in October! Fee, fi, fo, fum! I smell something! Let's after."

In about half an hour we have three well-defined lines of bees established,—two to farmhouses and one to the woods, and our box is being rapidly depleted of its honey. About every fourth bee goes to the woods, and now that they have learned the way thoroughly they do not make the long preliminary whirl above the box, but start directly from it. The woods are rough and dense and the hill steep, and we do not like to follow the line of bees until we have tried at least to settle the problem as to the distance they go into the woods,—whether the tree is on this side of the ridge or into the depth of the forest on the other side. So we shut up the box when it is full of bees and carry it about three hundred yards along the wall from which we are operating. When liberated, the bees, as they always will in such cases, go off in the same directions they have been going; they do not seem to know that they have been moved. But other bees have followed our scent, and it is not many minutes before a second line to the woods is established. This is called cross-lining the bees. The new line makes a sharp angle with the other line, and we know at once that the tree is only a few rods into the woods. The two lines we have established form two sides of a triangle of which the wall is the base; at the apex of the triangle, or where the two lines meet in the woods, we are sure to find the tree. We quickly follow up these lines, and where they cross each other on the side of the hill we scan every tree closely. I pause at the foot of an oak and examine a hole near the root; now the bees are in this tree and their entrance is on the upper side near the ground not two feet from the hole I peer into, and yet so quiet and secret is their going and coming that I fail to discover them and pass on up the hill. Failing in this direction I return to the oak again, and then perceive the bees going out in a small crack in the tree. The bees do not know they are found out and that the game is in our hands, and are as oblivious of our presence as if we were ants or crickets. The indications are that the swarm is a small one, and the store of honey trifling. In "taking up" a bee-tree it is usual first to kill or stupefy the bees with the fumes of burning sulphur or with tobacco smoke. But this course is impracticable on the present occasion, so we boldly and ruthlessly assault the tree with an axe we have procured. At the first blow the bees set up a loud buzzing, but we have no mercy, and the side of the cavity is soon cut away and the interior with its white-yellow mass of comb honey is exposed, and not a bee strikes a blow in defense of its all. This may seem singular, but it has nearly always been my experience. When a swarm of bees are thus rudely assaulted with an axe they evidently think the end of the world has come, and, like true misers as they are, each one seizes as much of the treasure as it can hold; in other words, they all fall to and gorge themselves with honey, and calmly await the issue. While in this condition they make no defense, and will not sting unless taken hold of. In fact they are as harmless as flies. Bees are always to be managed with boldness and decision. Any half-way measures, any timid poking about, any feeble attempts to reach their honey, are sure to be quickly resented. The popular notion that bees have a special antipathy toward certain persons and a liking for certain others has only this fact at the bottom of it: they will sting a person who is afraid of them and goes skulking and dodging about, and they will not sting a person who faces them boldly and has no dread of them. They are like dogs. The way to disarm a vicious dog is to show him you do not fear him; it is his turn to be afraid then. I never had any dread of bees and am seldom stung by them. I have climbed up into a large chestnut that contained a swarm in one of its cavities and chopped them out with an axe, being obliged at times to pause and brush the bewildered bees from my hands and face, and not been stung once. I have chopped a swarm out of an apple-tree in June, and taken out the cards of honey and arranged them in a hive, and then dipped out the bees with a dipper, and taken the whole home with me in pretty good condition, with scarcely any opposition on the part of the bees. In reaching your hand into the cavity to detach and remove the comb you are pretty sure to get stung, for when you touch the "business end" of a bee, it will sting even though its head be off. But the bee carries the antidote to its own poison. The best remedy for bee sting is honey, and when your hands are besmeared with honey, as they are sure to be on such occasions, the wound is scarcely more painful than the prick of a pin. Assault your bee-tree, then, boldly with your axe, and you will find that when the honey is exposed every bee has surrendered and the whole swarm is cowering in helpless bewilderment and terror. Our tree yields only a few pounds of honey, not enough to have lasted the swarm till January, but no matter: we have the less burden to carry.

In the afternoon we go nearly half a mile farther along the ridge to a cornfield that lies immediately in front of the highest point of the mountain. The view is superb; the ripe autumn landscape rolls away to the east, cut through by the great placid river; in the extreme north the wall of the Catskills stands out clear and strong, while in the south the mountains of the Highlands bound the view. The day is warm, and the bees are very busy there in that neglected corner of the field, rich in asters, fleabane, and goldenrod. The corn has been cut, and upon a stout but a few rods from the woods, which here drop quickly down from the precipitous heights, we set up our bee-box, touched again with the pungent oil. In a few moments a bee has found it; she comes up to leeward, following the scent. On leaving the box, she goes straight toward the woods. More bees quickly come, and it is not long before the line is well established. Now we have recourse to the same tactics we employed before, and move along the ridge to another field to get our cross line. But the bees still go in almost the same direction they did from the corn stout. The tree is then either on the top of the mountain or on the other or west side of it. We hesitate to make the plunge into the woods and seek to scale those precipices, for the eye can plainly see what is before us. As the afternoon sun gets lower, the bees are seen with wonderful distinctness. They fly toward and under the sun, and are in a strong light, while the near woods which form the background are in deep shadow. They look like large luminous motes. Their swiftly vibrating, transparent wings surround their bodies with a shining nimbus that makes them visible for a long distance. They seem magnified many times. We see them bridge the little gulf between us and the woods, then rise up over the treetops with their burdens, swerving neither to the right hand nor to the left. It is almost pathetic to see them labor so, climbing the mountain and unwittingly guiding us to their treasures. When the sun gets down so that his direction corresponds exactly with the course of the bees, we make the plunge. It proves even harder climbing than we had anticipated; the mountain is faced by a broken and irregular wall of rock, up which we pull ourselves slowly and cautiously by main strength. In half an hour, the perspiration streaming from every pore, we reach the summit. The trees here are all small, a second growth, and we are soon convinced the bees are not here. Then down we go on the other side, clambering down the rocky stairways till we reach quite a broad plateau that forms something like the shoulder of the mountain. On the brink of this there are many large hemlocks, and we scan them closely and rap upon them with our axe. But not a bee is seen or heard; we do not seem as near the tree as we were in the fields below; yet, if some divinity would only whisper the fact to us, we are within a few rods of the coveted prize, which is not in one of the large hemlocks or oaks that absorb our attention, but in an old stub or stump not six feet high, and which we have seen and passed several times without giving it a thought. We go farther down the mountain and beat about to the right and left, and get entangled in brush and arrested by precipices, and finally, as the day is nearly spent, give up the search and leave the woods quite baffled, but resolved to return on the morrow. The next day we come back and commence operations in an opening in the woods well down on the side of the mountain where we gave up the search. Our box is soon swarming with the eager bees, and they go back toward the summit we have passed. We follow back and establish a new line, where the ground will permit; then another and still another, and yet the riddle is not solved. One time we are south of them, then north, then the bees get up through the trees and we cannot tell where they go. But after much searching, and after the mystery seems rather to deepen than to clear up, we chance to pause beside the old stump. A bee comes out of a small opening like that made by ants in decayed wood, rubs its eyes and examines its antennæ, as bees always do before leaving their hive, then takes flight. At the same instant several bees come by us loaded with our honey and settle home with that peculiar low, complacent buzz of the well-filled insect. Here, then, is our idyl, our bit of Virgil and Theocritus, in a decayed stump of a hemlock tree. We could tear it open with our hands, and a bear would find it an easy prize, and a rich one, too, for we take from it fifty pounds of excellent honey. The bees have been here many years, and have of course sent out swarm after swarm into the wilds. They have protected themselves against the weather and strengthened their shaky habitation by a copious use of wax.

When a bee-tree is thus "taken up" in the middle of the day, of course a good many bees are away from home and have not heard the news. When they return and find the ground flowing with honey, and piles of bleeding combs lying about, they apparently do not recognize the place, and their first instinct is to fall to and fill themselves; this done, their next thought is to carry it home, so they rise up slowly through the branches of the trees till they have attained an altitude that enables them to survey the scene, when they seem to say, "Why, *this* is home," and down they come again; beholding the wreck and ruins once more, they still think there is some mistake, and get up a second or a third time and then drop back pitifully as before. It is the most pathetic sight of all, the surviving and bewildered bees struggling to save a few drops of their wasted treasures.

Presently, if there is another swarm in the woods, robber bees appear. You may know them by their saucy, chiding, devil-may-care hum. It is an ill wind that blows nobody good, and they make the most of the misfortune of their neighbors, and thereby pave the way for their own ruin. The hunter marks their course and the next day looks them up. On this occasion the day was hot and the honey very fragrant, and a line of bees was soon established S. S. W. Though there was much refuse honey in the old stub, and though little golden rills trickled down the hill from it, and the near branches and saplings were besmeared with it where we wiped our murderous hands, yet not a drop was wasted. It was a feast to which not only honey-bees came, but bumblebees, which at this season are hungry vagrants with no fixed place of abode, would gorge themselves, then creep beneath the bits of empty comb or fragments of bark and pass the night, and renew the feast next day. The bumblebee is an insect of which the bee-hunter sees much. There are all sorts and sizes of them. They are dull and clumsy compared with the honey-bee. Attracted in the fields by the bee-hunter's box, they will come up the wind on the scent and blunder into it in the most stupid, lubberly fashion.

The honey-bees that licked up our leavings on the old stub belonged to a swarm, as it proved, about half a mile farther down the ridge, and a few days afterward fate overtook them, and their stores in turn became the prey of another swarm in the vicinity, which also tempted Providence and were overwhelmed. The first-mentioned swarm I had lined from several points, and was following up the clew over rocks and through gulleys, when I came to where a large hemlock had been felled a few years before, and a swarm taken from a cavity near the top of it; fragments of the old comb were yet to be seen. A few yards away stood another short, squatty hemlock, and I said my bees ought to be there. As I paused near it, I noticed where the tree had been wounded with an axe a couple of feet from the ground many years before. The wound had partially grown over, but there was an opening there that I did not see at the first glance. I was about to pass on when a bee passed me making that peculiar shrill, discordant hum that a bee makes when besmeared with honey. I saw it alight in the partially closed wound and crawl home; then came others and others, little bands and squads of them heavily freighted with honey from the box. The tree was about twenty inches through and hollow at the butt, or from the axe-mark down. This space the bees had completely filled with honey. With an axe we cut away the outer ring of live wood and exposed the treasure. Despite the utmost care, we wounded the comb so that little rills of the golden liquid issued from the root of the tree and trickled down the hill.

The other bee-tree in the vicinity to which I have referred we found one warm November day in less than half an hour after entering the woods. It also was a hemlock that stood in a niche in a wall of hoary, moss-covered rocks thirty feet high. The tree hardly reached to the top of the precipice. The bees entered a small hole at the root, which was seven or eight feet from the ground. The position was a striking one. Never did apiary have a finer outlook or more rugged surroundings. A black, wood-embraced lake lay at our feet; the long panorama of the Catskills filled the far distance, and the more broken outlines of the Shawangunk range filled the rear. On every hand were precipices and a wild confusion of rocks and trees.

The cavity occupied by the bees was about three feet and a half long and eight or ten inches in diameter. With an axe we cut away one side of the tree, and laid bare its curiously wrought heart of honey. It was a most pleasing sight. What winding and devious ways the bees had through their palace! What great masses and blocks of snow-white comb there were! Where it was sealed up, presenting that slightly dented, uneven surface, it looked like some precious ore. When we carried a large pailful of it out of the woods it seemed still more like ore.

Your native bee-hunter predicates the distance of the tree by the time the bee occupies in making its first trip. But this is no certain guide. You are always safe in calculating that the tree is inside of a mile, and you need not as a rule look for your bee's return under ten minutes. One day I picked up a bee in an opening in the woods and gave it honey, and it made three trips to my box with an interval of about twelve minutes between them; it returned alone each time; the tree, which I afterward found, was about half a mile distant.

In lining bees through the woods the tactics of the hunter are to pause every twenty or thirty rods, lop away the branches or cut down the trees, and set the bees to work again. If they still go forward, he goes forward also and repeats his observations till the tree is found, or till the bees turn and come back upon the trail. Then he knows he has passed the tree, and he retraces his steps to a convenient distance and tries again, and thus quickly reduces the space to be looked over till the swarm is traced home. On one occasion, in a wild rocky wood, where the surface alternated between deep gulfs and chasms filled with thick, heavy growths of timber and sharp, precipitous, rocky ridges like a tempest-tossed sea, I carried my bees directly under their tree, and set them to work from a high, exposed ledge of rocks not thirty feet distant. One would have expected them under such circumstances to have gone straight home, as there were but few branches intervening, but they did not; they labored up through the trees and attained an altitude above the woods as if they had miles to travel, and thus baffled me for hours. Bees will always do this. They are acquainted with the woods only from the top side, and from the air above; they recognize home only by landmarks here, and in every instance they rise aloft to take their bearings. Think how familiar to them the topography of the forest summits must be,—an umbrageous sea or plain where every mark and point is known.

Another curious fact is that generally you will get track of a bee-tree sooner when you are half a mile from it than when you are only a few yards. Bees, like us human insects, have little faith in the near at hand; they expect to make their fortune in a distant field, they are lured by the remote and the difficult, and hence overlook the flower and the sweet at their very door. On several occasions I have unwittingly set my box within a few paces of a bee-tree and waited long for bees without getting them, when, on removing to a distant field or opening in the woods, I have got a clew at once.

I have a theory that when bees leave the hive, unless there is some special attraction in some other direction, they generally go against the wind. They would thus have the wind with them when they returned home heavily laden, and with these little navigators the difference is an important one. With a full cargo, a stiff head-wind is a great hindrance, but fresh and empty-handed they can face it with more ease. Virgil says bees bear gravel stones as ballast, but their only ballast is their honey-bag. Hence, when I go bee-hunting, I prefer to get to windward of the woods in which the swarm is supposed to have refuge.

Bees, like the milkman, like to be near a spring. They do water their honey, especially in a dry time. The liquid is then of course thicker and sweeter, and will bear diluting. Hence old bee-hunters look for bee-trees along creeks and near spring runs in the woods. I once found a tree a long distance from any water, and the honey had a peculiar bitter flavor, imparted to it, I was convinced, by rainwater sucked from the decayed and spongy hemlock-tree in which the swarm was found. In cutting into the tree, the north side of it was found to be saturated with water like a spring, which ran out in big drops, and had a bitter flavor. The bees had thus found a spring or a cistern in their own house.

Bees are exposed to many hardships and many dangers. Winds and storms prove as disastrous to them as to other navigators. Black spiders lie in wait for them as do brigands for travelers. One day, as I was looking for a bee amid some goldenrod, I spied one partly concealed under a leaf. Its baskets were full of pollen, and it did not move. On lifting up the leaf I discovered that a hairy spider was ambushed there and had the bee by the throat. The vampire was evidently afraid of the bee's sting, and was holding it by the throat till quite sure of its death. Virgil speaks of the painted lizard, perhaps a species of salamander, as an enemy of the honey-bee. We have no lizard that destroys the bee; but our tree-toad, ambushed among the apple and cherry blossoms, snaps them up wholesale. Quick as lightning that subtle but clammy tongue darts forth, and the unsuspecting bee is gone. Virgil also accuses the titmouse and the woodpecker of preying upon the bees, and our kingbird has been charged with the like crime, but the latter devours only the drones. The workers are either too small and quick for it or else it dreads their sting.

Virgil, by the way, had little more than a child's knowledge of the honey-bee. There is little fact and much fable in his fourth Georgic. If he had ever kept bees himself, or even visited an apiary, it is hard to see how he could have believed that the bee in its flight abroad carried a gravel stone for ballast.

"And as when empty barks on billows float,
   With sandy ballast sailors trim the boat;
   So bees bear gravel stones, whose poising weight
   Steers through the whistling winds their steady flight";

or that, when two colonies made war upon each other, they issued forth from their hives led by their kings and fought in the air, strewing the ground with the dead and dying:—

"Hard hailstones lie not thicker on the plain,
      Nor shaken oaks such show'rs of acorns rain."

It is quite certain he had never been bee-hunting. If he had we should have had a fifth Georgic. Yet he seems to have known that bees sometimes escaped to the woods:

"Nor bees are lodged in hives alone, but found
      In chambers of their own beneath the ground:

Their vaulted roofs are hung in pumices,
And in the rotten trunks of hollow trees."

Wild honey is as near like tame as wild bees are like their brothers in the hive. The only difference is, that wild honey is flavored with your adventure, which makes it a little more delectable than the domestic article.

A SNOW-STORM

That is a striking line with which Emerson opens his beautiful poem of the Snow-Storm—

"Announced by all the trumpets of the sky,
  Arrives the snow, and, driving o'er the fields,
  Seems nowhere to alight."

One seems to see the clouds puffing their cheeks as they sound the charge of their white legions. But the line is more accurately descriptive of a rain-storm, as, in both summer and winter, rain is usually preceded by wind. Homer, describing a snow-storm in his time, says:—

"The winds are lulled."

The preparations of a snow-storm are, as a rule, gentle and quiet; a marked hush pervades both the earth and the sky. The movements of the celestial forces are muffled, as if the snow already paved the way of their coming. There is no uproar, no clashing of arms, no blowing of wind trumpets. These soft, feathery, exquisite crystals are formed as if in the silence and

privacy of the inner cloud-chambers. Rude winds would break
the spell and mar the process. The clouds are smoother, and
slower in their movements, with less definite outlines than those
which bring rain. In fact, everything is prophetic of the gentle
and noiseless meteor that is approaching, and of the stillness
that is to succeed it, when "all the batteries of sound are
spiked," as Lowell says, and "we see the movements of life
as a deaf man sees it,—a mere wraith of the clamorous exis-
tence that inflicts itself on our ears when the ground is bare."
After the storm is fairly launched, the winds not infrequently
awake, and, seeing their opportunity, pipe the flakes a lively
dance. I am speaking now of the typical, full-born midwinter
storm that comes to us from the North or N. N. E., and that
piles the landscape knee-deep with snow. Such a storm once
came to us the last day of January,—the master-storm of the
winter. Previous to that date, we had had but light snow. The
spruces had been able to catch it all upon their arms, and keep
a circle of bare ground beneath them where the birds scratched.
But the day following this fall, they stood with their lower
branches completely buried. If the Old Man of the North had
but sent us his couriers and errand-boys before, the old gray-
beard appeared himself at our doors on this occasion, and we
were all his subjects. His flag was upon every tree and roof,
his seal upon every door and window, and his embargo upon
every path and highway. He slipped down upon us, too, under
the cover of such a bright, seraphic day,—a day that disarmed
suspicion with all but the wise ones, a day without a cloud or
a film, a gentle breeze from the west, a dry, bracing air, a
blazing sun that brought out the bare ground under the lee of
the fences and farm-buildings, and at night a spotless moon
near her full. The next morning the sky reddened in the east,

then became gray, heavy, and silent. A seamless cloud covered
it. The smoke from the chimneys went up with a barely perceptible slant toward the north. In the forenoon the cedar-
birds, purple finches, yellowbirds, nuthatches, bluebirds, were
in flocks or in couples and trios about the trees, more or less
noisy and loquacious. About noon a thin white veil began to
blur the distant southern mountains. It was like a white dream
slowly descending upon them. The first flake or flakelet that
reached me was a mere white speck that came idly circling
and eddying to the ground. I could not see it after it alighted.
It might have been a scale from the feather of some passing
bird, or a larger mote in the air that the stillness was allowing
to settle. Yet it was the altogether inaudible and infinitesimal
trumpeter that announced the coming storm, the grain of sand
that heralded the desert. Presently another fell, then another;
the white mist was creeping up the river valley. How slowly
and loiteringly it came, and how microscopic its first siftings!

This mill is bolting its flour very fine, you think. But wait
a little; it gets coarser by and by; you begin to see the flakes;
they increase in numbers and in size, and before one o'clock
it is snowing steadily. The flakes come straight down, but in
a half hour they have a marked slant toward the north; the
wind is taking a hand in the game. By mid-afternoon the storm
is coming in regular pulse-beats or in vertical waves. The wind
is not strong, but seems steady; the pines hum, yet there is a
sort of rhythmic throb in the meteor; the air toward the wind
looks ribbed with steady-moving vertical waves of snow. The
impulses travel along like undulations in a vast suspended
white curtain, imparted by some invisible hand there in the
northeast. As the day declines the storm waxes, the wind
increases, the snow-fall thickens, and

> "the housemates sit
> Around the radiant fireplace, inclosed
> In a tumultuous privacy of storm,"

a privacy which you feel outside as well as in. Out-of-doors you seem in a vast tent of snow; the distance is shut out, near-by objects are hidden; there are white curtains above you and white screens about you, and you feel housed and secluded in storm. Your friend leaves your door, and he is wrapped away in white obscurity, caught up in a cloud, and his footsteps are obliterated. Travelers meet on the road, and do not see or hear each other till they are face to face. The passing train, half a mile away, gives forth a mere wraith of sound. Its whistle is deadened as in a dense wood.

Still the storm rose. At five o'clock I went forth to face it in a two-mile walk. It was exhilarating in the extreme. The snow was lighter than chaff. It had been dried in the Arctic ovens to the last degree. The foot sped through it without hindrance. I fancied the grouse and quails quietly sitting down in the open places, and letting it drift over them. With head under wing, and wing snugly folded, they would be softly and tenderly buried in a few moments. The mice and the squirrels were in their dens, but I fancied the fox asleep upon some rock or log, and allowing the flakes to cover him. The hare in her form, too, was being warmly sepulchred with the rest. I thought of the young cattle and the sheep huddled together on the lee side of a haystack in some remote field, all enveloped in mantles of white.

> "I thought me on the ourie cattle,
> Or silly sheep, wha bide this brattle
> O' wintry war,

Or thro' the drift, deep-lairing sprattle,
  Beneath a scaur.

"Ilk happing bird, wee helpless thing,
That in the merry months o' spring
Delighted me to hear thee sing,
  What comes o' thee?
Where wilt thou cow'r thy chittering wing,
  And close thy ee?"

As I passed the creek, I noticed the white woolly masses that filled the water. It was as if somebody upstream had been washing his sheep and the water had carried away all the wool, and I thought of the Psalmist's phrase, "He giveth snow like wool." On the river a heavy fall of snow simulates a thin layer of cotton batting. The tide drifts it along, and, where it meets with an obstruction alongshore, it folds up and becomes wrinkled or convoluted like a fabric, or like cotton sheeting. Attempt to row a boat through it, and it seems indeed like cotton or wool, every fibre of which resists your progress.

As the sun went down and darkness fell, the storm impulse reached its full. It became a wild conflagration of wind and snow; the world was wrapt in frost flame; it enveloped one, and penetrated his lungs and caught away his breath like a blast from a burning city. How it whipped around and under every cover and searched out every crack and crevice, sifting under the shingles in the attic, darting its white tongue under the kitchen door, puffing its breath down the chimney, roaring through the woods, stalking like a sheeted ghost across the hills, bending in white and ever-changing forms above the fences, sweeping across the plains, whirling in eddies behind the buildings, or leaping spitefully up their walls,—in short, taking the world entirely to itself, and giving a loose rein to its desire.

But in the morning, behold! the world was not consumed; it was not the besom of destruction, after all, but the gentle hand of mercy. How deeply and warmly and spotlessly Earth's nakedness is clothed!—the "wool" of the Psalmist nearly two feet deep. And as far as warmth and protection are concerned, there is a good deal of the virtue of wool in such a snow-fall. How it protects the grass, the plants, the roots of the trees, and the worms, insects, and smaller animals in the ground! It is a veritable fleece, beneath which the shivering earth ("the frozen hills ached with pain," says one of our young poets) is restored to warmth. When the temperature of the air is at zero, the thermometer, placed at the surface of the ground beneath a foot and a half of snow, would probably indicate but a few degrees below freezing; the snow is rendered such a perfect non-conductor of heat mainly by reason of the quantity of air that is caught and retained between the crystals. Then how, like a fleece of wool, it rounds and fills out the landscape, and makes the leanest and most angular field look smooth!

The day dawned, and continued as innocent and fair as the day which had preceded,—two mountain-peaks of sky and sun, with their valley of cloud and snow between. Walk to the nearest spring run on such a morning, and you can see the Colorado valley and the great cañons of the West in miniature, carved in alabaster. In the midst of the plain of snow lie these chasms; the vertical walls, the bold headlands, the turrets and spires and obelisks, the rounded and towering capes, the carved and buttressed precipices, the branch valleys and cañ- ons, and the winding and tortuous course of the main channel are all here,—all that the Yosemite or Yellowstone have to

show, except the terraces and the cascades. Sometimes my
cañon is bridged, and one's fancy runs nimbly across a vast
arch of Parian marble, and that makes up for the falls and the
terraces. Where the ground is marshy, I come upon a pretty
and vivid illustration of what I have read and been told of the
Florida formation. This white and brittle limestone is under-
mined by water. Here are the dimples and depressions, the
sinks and the wells, the springs and the lakes. Some places a
mouse might break through the surface and reveal the water
far beneath, or the snow gives way of its own weight, and you
have a minute Florida well, with the truncated cone-shape and
all. The arched and subterranean pools and passages are there
likewise.

But there is a more beautiful and fundamental geology than
this in the snow-storm: we are admitted into Nature's oldest
laboratory, and see the working of the law by which the foundations of the material universe were laid,—the law or mystery
of crystallization. The earth is built upon crystals; the granite
rock is only a denser and more compact snow, or a kind of ice
that was vapor once and may be vapor again. "Every stone is
nothing else but a congealed lump of frozen earth," says Plu-
tarch. By cold and pressure air can be liquefied, perhaps
solidified. A little more time, a little more heat, and the hills
are but April snow-banks. Nature has but two forms, the cell
and the crystal,—the crystal first, the cell last. All organic
nature is built up of the cell; all inorganic, of the crystal.
Cell upon cell rises the vegetable, rises the animal; crystal wedded
to and compacted with crystal stretches the earth beneath them.
See in the falling snow the old cooling and precipitation, and
the shooting, radiating forms that are the architects of planet
and globe.

We love the sight of the brown and ruddy earth; it is the color of life, while a snow-covered plain is the face of death; yet snow is but the mask of the life-giving rain; it, too, is the friend of man,—the tender, sculpturesque, immaculate, warming, fertilizing snow.

WILD LIFE ABOUT
MY CABIN

Friends have often asked me why I turned my back upon the Hudson and retreated into the wilderness. Well, I do not call it a retreat; I call it a withdrawal, a retirement, the taking up of a new position to renew the attack, it may be, more vigorously than ever. It is not always easy to give reasons. There are reasons within reasons, and often no reasons at all that we are aware of.

To a countryman like myself, not born to a great river or an extensive water-view, these things, I think, grow wearisome after a time. He becomes surfeited with a beauty that is alien to him. He longs for something more homely, private, and secluded. Scenery may be too fine or too grand and imposing for one's daily and hourly view. It tires after a while. It demands a mood that comes to you only at intervals. Hence it is never wise to build your house on the most ambitious spot in the landscape. Rather seek out a more humble and secluded nook or corner, which you can fill and warm with your domestic and home instincts and affections. In some things the half is often more satisfying than the whole. A glimpse of the Hudson River between hills or through openings in the trees wears better with me than a long expanse of it constantly spread out before me. One day I had an errand to a farmhouse nestled in a little valley or basin at the foot of a mountain. The earth put out protecting arms all about it,—a low hill with an orchard on one side, a sloping pasture on another, and the mountain, with the skirts of its mantling forests, close at hand in the rear. How my heart warmed toward it! I had been so long perched high upon the banks of a great river, in sight of all the world, exposed to every wind that blows, with a horizon-line that sweeps over half a county, that, quite unconsciously to myself, I was pining for a nook to sit down in. I was hungry for the private and the circumscribed; I knew it when I saw this sheltered farmstead. I had long been restless and dissatisfied,— a vague kind of homesickness; now I knew the remedy. Hence when, not long afterward, I was offered a tract of wild land, barely a mile from home, that contained a secluded nook and a few acres of level, fertile land shut off from the vain and noisy world of railroads, steamboats, and yachts by a wooded, precipitous mountain, I quickly closed the bargain, and built me a rustic house there, which I call "Slabsides," because its outer walls are covered with slabs. I might have given it a prettier name, but not one more fit, or more in keeping with the mood that brought me thither. A slab is the first cut from the log, and the bark goes with it. It is like the first cut from the loaf, which we call the crust, and which the children reject, but which we older ones often prefer. I wanted to take a fresh cut of life,—something that had the bark on, or, if you please, that was like a well-browned and hardened crust. After three years I am satisfied with the experiment. Life has a different flavor here. It is reduced to simpler terms; its complex equations all disappear. The exact value of x may still elude me, but I can press it hard; I have shorn it of many of its disguises and entanglements.

When I went into the woods the robins went with me, or rather they followed close. As soon as a space of ground was cleared and the garden planted, they were on hand to pick up the worms and insects, and to superintend the planting of the cherry-trees: three pairs the first summer, and more than double that number the second. In the third, their early morning chorus was almost as marked a feature as it is about the old farm homesteads. The robin is no hermit: he likes company; he likes the busy scenes of the farm and the village; he likes to carol to listening ears, and to build his nest as near your dwelling as he can. Only at rare intervals do I find a real sylvan robin, one that nests in the woods, usually by still waters, remote from human habitation. In such places his morning and evening carol is a welcome surprise to the fisherman or camper-out. It is like a dooryard flower found blooming in the wilderness. With the robins came the song sparrows and social sparrows, or chippies, also. The latter nested in the bushes near my cabin, and the song sparrows in the bank above the ditch that drains my land. I notice that Chippy finds just as many horsehairs to weave into her nest here in my horseless domain as she does when she builds in the open country. Her partiality for the long hairs from the manes and tails of horses and cattle is so great that she is often known as the hair-bird. What would she do in a country where there were neither cows nor horses? Yet these hairs are not good nesting-material. They are slippery, refractory things, and occasionally cause a tragedy in the nest by getting looped around the legs or the neck of the young or of the parent bird. They probably give a smooth finish to the interior, dear to the heart of Chippy.

The first year of my cabin life a pair of robins attempted to build a nest upon the round timber that forms the plate under my porch roof. But it was a poor place to build in. It took nearly a week's time and caused the birds a great waste of labor to find this out. The coarse material they brought for the foundation would not bed well upon the rounded surface of the timber, and every vagrant breeze that came along swept it off. My porch was kept littered with twigs and weed-stalks for days, till finally the birds abandoned the undertaking. The next season a wiser or more experienced pair made the attempt again, and succeeded. They placed the nest against the rafter where it joins the plate; they used mud from the start to level up with and to hold the first twigs and straws, and had soon completed a firm, shapely structure. When the young were about ready to fly, it was interesting to note that there was apparently an older and a younger, as in most families. One bird was more advanced than any of the others. Had the parent birds intentionally stimulated it with extra quantities of food, so as to be able to launch their offspring into the world one at a time? At any rate, one of the birds was ready to leave the nest a day and a half before any of the others. I happened to be looking at it when the first impulse to get outside the nest seemed to seize it. Its parents were encouraging it with calls and assurances from some rocks a few yards away. It answered their calls in vigorous, strident tones. Then it climbed over the edge of the nest upon the plate, took a few steps forward, then a few more, till it was a yard from the nest and near the end of the timber, and could look off into free space. Its parents apparently shouted, "Come on!" But its courage was not quite equal to the leap; it looked around, and seeing how far it was from home, scampered back to the nest, and climbed into it like a frightened child. It had made its first journey into the world, but the home tie had brought it quickly back. A few hours afterward it journeyed to the end of the plate again, and then turned and rushed back. The third time its heart was braver, its wings stronger, and leaping into the air with a shout, it flew easily to some rocks a dozen or more yards away. Each of the young in succession, at intervals of nearly a day, left the nest in this manner. There would be the first journey of a few feet along the plate, the first sudden panic at being so far from home, the rush back, a second and perhaps a third attempt, and then the irrevocable leap into the air, and a clamorous flight to a near-by bush or rock. Young birds never go back when they have once taken flight. The first free flap of the wing severs forever the ties that bind them to home.

The chickadees we have always with us. They are like the evergreens among the trees and plants. Winter has no terrors for them. They are properly wood-birds, but the groves and orchards know them also. Did they come near my cabin for better protection, or did they chance to find a little cavity in a tree there that suited them? Branch-builders and ground-builders are easily accommodated, but the chickadee must find a cavity, and a small one at that. The woodpeckers make a cavity when a suitable trunk or branch is found, but the chickadee, with its small, sharp beak, rarely does so; it usually smooths and deepens one already formed. This a pair did a few yards from my cabin. The opening was into the heart of a little sassafras, about four feet from the ground. Day after day the birds took turns in deepening and enlarging the cavity: a soft, gentle hammering for a few moments in the heart of the little tree, and then the appearance of the worker at the opening, with the chips in his, or her, beak. They changed off every little while, one working while the other gathered food. Absolute equality of the sexes, both in plumage and in duties, seems to prevail among these birds, as among a few other species. During the preparations for housekeeping the birds were hourly seen and heard, but as soon as the first egg was laid, all this was changed. They suddenly became very shy and quiet. Had it not been for the new egg that was added each day, one would have concluded that they had abandoned the place. There was a precious secret now that must be well kept. After incubation began, it was only by watching that I could get a glimpse of one of the birds as it came quickly to feed or to relieve the other.

One day a lot of Vassar girls came to visit me, and I led them out to the little sassafras to see the chickadees' nest. The sitting bird kept her place as head after head, with its nodding plumes and millinery, appeared above the opening to her chamber, and a pair of inquisitive eyes peered down upon her. But I saw that she was getting ready to play her little trick to frighten them away. Presently I heard a faint explosion at the bottom of the cavity, when the peeping girl jerked her head quickly back, with the exclamation, "Why, it spit at me!" The trick of the bird on such occasions is apparently to draw in its breath till its form perceptibly swells, and then give forth a quick, explosive sound like an escaping jet of steam. One involuntarily closes his eyes and jerks back his head. The girls, to their great amusement, provoked the bird into this pretty outburst of her impatience two or three times. But as the ruse failed of its effect, the bird did not keep it up, but let the laughing faces gaze till they were satisfied.

There is only one other bird known to me that resorts to the same trick to scare away intruders, and that is the great crested flycatcher. As your head appears before the entrance to the cavity in which the mother bird is sitting, a sudden burst of escaping steam seems directed at your face, and your backward movement leaves the way open for the bird to escape, which she quickly does.

The chickadee is a prolific bird, laying from six to eight eggs, and it seems to have few natural enemies. I think it is seldom molested by squirrels or black snakes or weasels or crows or owls. The entrance to the nest is usually so small that none of these creatures can come at them. Yet the number of chickadees in any given territory seems small. What keeps them in check? Probably the rigors of winter and a limited food-supply. The ant-eaters, fruit-eaters, and seed-eaters mostly migrate. Our all-the-year-round birds, like the chickadees, woodpeckers, jays, and nuthatches, live mostly on nuts and the eggs and larvæ of tree-insects, and hence their larder is a restricted one; hence, also, these birds rear only one brood in a season. A hairy woodpecker passed the winter in the woods near me by subsisting on a certain small white grub which he found in the bark of some dead hemlock-trees. He "worked" these trees,—four of them,—as the slang is, "for all they were worth." The grub was under the outer shell of bark, and the bird literally skinned the trees in getting at his favorite morsel. He worked from the top downward, hammering or prying off this shell, and leaving the trunk of the tree with a red, denuded look. Bushels of the fragments of the bark covered the ground at the foot of the tree in spring, and the trunk looked as if it had been flayed,—as it had.

The big chimney of my cabin of course attracted the chimney swifts, and as it was not used in summer, two pairs built their nests in it, and we had the muffled thunder of their wings at all hours of the day and night. One night, when one of the broods was nearly fledged, the nest that held them fell down into the fireplace. Such a din of screeching and chattering as they instantly set up! Neither my dog nor I could sleep. They yelled in chorus, stopping at the end of every half-minute as if upon signal. Now they were all screeching at the top of their voices, then a sudden, dead silence ensued. Then the din began again, to terminate at the instant as before. If they had been long practicing together, they could not have succeeded better. I never before heard the cry of birds so accurately timed. After a while I got up and put them back up the chimney, and stopped up the throat of the flue with newspapers. The next day one of the parent birds, in bringing food to them, came down the chimney with such force that it passed through the papers and brought up in the fireplace. On capturing it I saw that its throat was distended with food as a chipmunk's cheek with corn, or a boy's pocket with chestnuts. I opened its mandibles, when it ejected a wad of insects as large as a bean. Most of them were much macerated, but there were two house-flies yet alive and but little the worse for their close confinement. They stretched themselves, and walked about upon my hand, enjoying a breath of fresh air once more. It was nearly two hours before the swift again ventured into the chimney with food.

These birds do not perch, nor alight upon buildings or the ground. They are apparently upon the wing all day. They outride the storms. I have in my mind a cheering picture of three of them I saw facing a heavy thunder-shower one afternoon. The wind was blowing a gale, the clouds were rolling in black, portentous billows out of the west, the peals of thunder were shaking the heavens, and the big drops were just beginning to come down, when, on looking up, I saw three swifts high in air, working their way slowly, straight into the teeth of the storm. They were not hurried or disturbed; they held themselves firmly and steadily; indeed, they were fairly at anchor in the air till the rage of the elements should have subsided. I do not know that any other of our land birds outride the storms in this way.

The phœbe-birds also soon found me out in my retreat, and a pair of them deliberated a long while about building on a little shelf in one of my gables. But, much to my regret, they finally decided in favor of a niche in the face of a ledge of rocks not far from my spring. The place was well screened by bushes and well guarded against the approach of snakes or four-footed prowlers, and the birds prospered well and reared two broods. They have now occupied the same nest three years in succession. This is unusual: Phœbe prefers a new nest each season, but in this case there is no room for another, and, the site being a choice one, she slightly repairs and refurnishes her nest each spring, leaving the new houses for her more ambitious neighbors.

Of wood-warblers my territory affords many specimens. One spring a solitary Nashville warbler lingered near my cabin for a week. I heard his bright, ringing song at all hours of the day. The next spring there were two or more, and they nested in my pea-bushes. The black and white creeping warblers are perhaps the most abundant. A pair of them built a nest in a steep moss and lichen covered hillside, beside a high gray rock. Our path to Julian's Rock led just above it. It was an ideal spot and an ideal nest, but it came to grief. Some small creature sucked the eggs. On removing the nest I found an earth-stained egg beneath it. Evidently the egg had ripened before its receptacle was ready, and the mother, for good luck, had placed it in the foundation.

One day, as I sat at my table writing, I had a call from the worm-eating warbler. It came into the open door, flitted about inquisitively, and then, startled by the apparition at the table, dashed against the window-pane and fell down stunned. I picked it up, and it lay with closed eyes panting in my hand. I carried it into the open air. In a moment or two it opened its eyes, looked about, and then closed them and fell to panting again. Soon it looked up at me once more and about the room, and seemed to say: "Where am I? What has happened to me?" Presently the panting ceased, the bird's breathing became more normal, it gradually got its bearings, and, at a motion of my hand, darted away. This is an abundant warbler in my vicinity, and nested this year near by. I have discovered that it has an air-song—the song of ecstasy—like that of the oven-bird. I had long suspected it, as I frequently heard a fine burst of melody that was new to me. One June day I was fortunate enough to see the bird delivering its song in the air above the low trees. As with the oven-bird, its favorite hour is the early twilight, though I hear the song occasionally at other hours. The bird darts upward fifty feet or more, about half the height that the oven-bird attains, and gives forth a series of rapid, ringing musical notes, which quickly glide into the long, sparrow-like trill that forms its ordinary workaday song. While this part is being uttered, the singer is on its downward flight into the woods. The flight-song of the oven-bird is louder and more striking, and is not so shy and furtive a performance. The latter I hear many times every June twilight, and I frequently see the singer reach his climax a hundred feet or more in the air, and then mark his arrow-like flight downward. I have heard this song also in the middle of the night near my cabin. At such times it stands out on the stillness like a bursting rocket on the background of the night.

One or two mornings in April, at a very early hour, I am quite sure to hear the hermit thrush singing in the bushes near my window. How quickly I am transported to the Delectable Mountains and to the mossy solitudes of the northern woods! The winter wren also pauses briefly in his northern journey, and surprises and delights my ear with his sudden lyrical burst of melody. Such a dapper, fidgety, gesticulating, bobbing-up-and-down-and-out-and-in little bird, and yet full of such sweet, wild melody! To get him at his best, one needs to hear him in a dim, northern hemlock wood, where his voice reverberates as in a great hall; just as one should hear the veery in a beech and birch wood, beside a purling trout brook, when the evening shades are falling. It then becomes to you the voice of some particular spirit of the place and the hour. The veery does not inhabit the woods immediately about my cabin, but in the summer twilight he frequently comes up from the valley below and sings along the borders of my territory. How welcome his simple flute-like strain! The wood thrush is the leading chorister in the woods about me. He does not voice the wildness, but seems to give a touch of something half rural, half urban,—such is the power of association in bird-songs. In the evening twilight I often sit on the highest point of the rocky rim of the great granite bowl that holds my three acres of prairie soil, and see the shadows deepen, and listen to the bird voices that rise up from the forest below me. The songs of many wood thrushes make a sort of golden warp in the texture of sounds that is being woven about me. Now the flight-song of the oven-bird holds the ear, then the fainter one of the worm-eating warbler lures it. The carol of the robin, the vesper hymn of the tanager, the flute of the veery, are all on the air. Finally, as the shadows deepen and the stars begin to come out, the whip-poor-will suddenly strikes up. What a rude intrusion upon the serenity and harmony of the hour! A cry without music, insistent, reiterated, loud, penetrating, and yet the ear welcomes it also; the night and the solitude are so vast that they can stand it; and when, an hour later, as the night enters into full possession, the bird comes and serenades me under my window or upon my doorstep, my heart warms toward it. Its cry is a love-call, and there is something of the ardor and persistence of love in it, and when the female responds, and comes and hovers near, there is an interchange of subdued, caressing tones between the two birds that it is a delight to hear. During my first summer here one bird used to strike up every night from a high ledge of rocks in front of my door. At just such a moment in the twilight he would begin, the first to break the stillness. Then the others would follow, till the solitude was vocal with their calls. They are rarely heard later than ten o'clock. Then at daybreak they take up the tale again, whipping poor Will till one pities him. One April morning between three and four o'clock, hearing one strike up near my window, I began counting its calls. My neighbor had told me he had heard one call over two hundred times without a break, which seemed to me a big story. But I have a much bigger one to tell. This bird actually laid upon the back of poor Will one thousand and eighty-eight blows, with only a barely perceptible pause here and there, as if to catch its breath. Then it stopped about half a minute and began again, uttering this time three hundred and ninety calls, when it paused, flew a little farther away, took up the tale once more, and continued till I fell asleep.

By day the whip-poor-will apparently sits motionless upon the ground. A few times in my walks through the woods I have started one up from almost under my feet. On such occasions the bird's movements suggest those of a bat; its wings make no noise, and it wavers about in an uncertain manner, and quickly drops to the ground again. One June day we flushed an old one with her two young, but there was no indecision or hesitation in the manner of the mother bird this time. The young were more than half fledged, and they scampered away a few yards and suddenly squatted upon the ground, where their protective coloring rendered them almost invisible. Then the anxious parent put forth all her arts to absorb our attention and lure us away from her offspring. She flitted before us from side to side, with spread wings and tail, now falling upon the ground, where she would remain a moment as if quite disabled, then perching upon an old stump or low branch with drooping, quivering wings, and imploring us by every gesture to take her and spare her young. My companion had his camera with him, but the bird would not remain long enough in one position for him to get her picture. The whip-poor-will builds no nest, but lays her two blunt, speckled eggs upon the dry leaves, where the plumage of the sitting bird blends perfectly with her surroundings. The eye, only a few feet away, has to search long and carefully to make her out. Every gray and brown and black tint of dry leaf and lichen, and bit of bark or broken twig, is

copied in her plumage. In a day or two, after the young are
hatched, the mother begins to move about with them through
the woods.

When I want the wild of a little different flavor and quality
from that immediately about my cabin, I go a mile through the
woods to Black Creek, here called the Shattega, and put my
canoe into a long, smooth, silent stretch of water that winds
through a heavily timbered marsh till it leads into Black Pond,
an oval sheet of water half a mile or more across. Here I get
the moist, spongy, tranquil, luxurious side of Nature. Here
she stands or sits knee-deep in water, and wreathes herself
with pond-lilies in summer, and bedecks herself with scarlet
maples in autumn. She is an Indian maiden, dark, subtle,
dreaming, with glances now and then that thrill the wild blood
in one's veins. The Shattega here is a stream without banks
and with a just perceptible current. It is a waterway through
a timbered marsh. The level floor of the woods ends in an
irregular line where the level surface of the water begins. As
one glides along in his boat, he sees various rank aquatic
growths slowly waving in the shadowy depths beneath him.
The larger trees on each side unite their branches above his
head, so that at times he seems to be entering an arboreal cave
out of which glides the stream. In the more open places the
woods mirror themselves in the glassy surface till one seems
floating between two worlds, clouds and sky and trees below
him matching those around and above him. A bird flits from
shore to shore, and one sees it duplicated against the sky in
the under-world. What vistas open! What banks of drooping
foliage, what grain and arch of gnarled branches, lure the eye
as one drifts or silently paddles along! The stream has absorbed
the shadows so long that it is itself like a liquid shadow. Its

bed is lined with various dark vegetable growths, as with the skin of some huge, shaggy animal, the fur of which slowly stirs in the languid current. I go here in early spring, after the ice has broken up, to get a glimpse of the first wild ducks and to play the sportsman without a gun. I am sure I would not exchange the quiet surprise and pleasure I feel, as, on rounding some point or curve in the stream, two or more ducks spring suddenly out from some little cove or indentation in the shore, and with an alarum *quack, quack,* launch into the air and quickly gain the free spaces above the treetops, for the satisfaction of the gunner who sees their dead bodies fall before his murderous fire. He has only a dead duck, which, the chances are, he will not find very toothsome at this season, while I have a live duck with whistling wings cleaving the air northward, where, in some lake or river of Maine or Canada, in late summer, I may meet him again with his brood. It is so easy, too, to bag the game with your eye, while your gun may leave you only a feather or two floating upon the water. The duck has wit, and its wit is as quick as, or quicker than, the sportsman's gun. One day in spring I saw a gunner cut down a duck when it had gained an altitude of thirty or forty feet above the stream. At the report it stopped suddenly, turned a somersault, and fell with a splash into the water. It fell like a brick, and disappeared like one; only a feather and a few bubbles marked the spot where it struck. Had it sunk? No; it had dived. It was probably winged, and in the moment it occupied in falling to the water it had decided what to do. It would go beneath the hunter, since it could not escape above him; it could fly in the water with only one wing, with its feet to aid it. The gunner instantly set up a diligent search in all directions, up and down along the shores, peering long and

intently into the depths, thrusting his oar into the weeds and
driftwood at the edge of the water, but no duck or sign of duck
could he find. It was as if the wounded bird had taken to the
mimic heaven that looked so sunny and real down there, and
gone on to Canada by that route. What astonished me was that
the duck should have kept its presence of mind under such
trying circumstances, and not have lost a fraction of a second
of time in deciding on a course of action. The duck, I am
convinced, has more sagacity than any other of our commoner
fowl.

The day I see the first ducks I am pretty sure to come upon
the first flock of blackbirds,—rusty grackles,—resting awhile
on their northward journey amid the reeds, alders, and spice-
bush beside the stream. They allow me to approach till I can
see their yellow eyes and the brilliant iris on the necks and
heads of the males. Many of them are vocal, and their united
voices make a volume of sound that is analogous to a bundle
of slivers. Sputtering, splintering, rasping, rending, their notes
chafe and excite the ear. They suggest thorns and briers of
sound, and yet are most welcome. What voice that rises from
our woods or beside our waters in April is not tempered or
attuned to the ear? Just as I like to chew the crinkleroot and
the twigs of the spice-bush at this time, or at any time, for
that matter, so I like to treat my ear to these more aspirated
and astringent bird voices. Is it Thoreau who says they are
like pepper and salt to this sense? In all the blackbirds we
hear the voice of April not yet quite articulate; there is a
suggestion of catarrh and influenza still in the air-passages. I
should, perhaps, except the red-shouldered starling, whose
clear and liquid *gur-ga-lee* or *o-ka-lee*, above the full water-
courses, makes a different impression. The cowbird also has

a clear note, but it seems to be wrenched or pumped up with much effort.

In May I go to Black Creek to hear the warblers and the water-thrushes. It is the only locality where I have ever heard the two water-thrushes, or accentors, singing at the same time,—the New York and the large-billed. The latter is much more abundant and much the finer songster. How he does make these watery solitudes ring with his sudden, brilliant burst of song! But the more northern species pleases the ear also with his quieter and less hurried strain. I drift in my boat and let the ear attend to the one, then to the other, while the eye takes note of their quick, nervous movements and darting flight. The smaller species probably does not nest along this stream, but the large-billed breeds here abundantly. The last nest I found was in the roots of an upturned tree, with the water immediately beneath it. I had asked a neighboring farm-boy if he knew of any birds' nests.

"Yes," he said; and he named over the nests of robins, highholes, sparrows, and others, and then that of a "tip-up."

At this last I pricked up my ears, so to speak. I had not seen a tip-up's nest in many a day. "Where?" I inquired.

"In the roots of a tree in the woods," said Charley.

"Not the nest of the 'tip-up,' or sandpiper," said I. "It builds on the ground in the open country near streams."

"Anyhow, it tipped," replied the boy.

He directed me to the spot, and I found, as I expected to find, the nest of the water-thrush. When the Vassar girls came again, I conducted them to the spot, and they took turns in walking a small tree trunk above the water, and gazing upon a nest brimming with the downy backs of young birds.

When I am listening to the water-thrushes, I am also noting

with both eye and ear the warblers and vireos. There comes a week in May when the speckled Canada warblers are in the ascendant. They feed in the low bushes near the water's edge, and are very brisk and animated in voice and movement. The eye easily notes their slate-blue backs and yellow breasts with their broad band of black spots, and the ear quickly discriminates their not less marked and emphatic song.

In late summer I go to the Shattega, and to the lake out of which it flows, for white pond-lilies, and to feast my eye on the masses of purple loosestrife and the more brilliant but more hidden and retired cardinal-flower that bloom upon its banks. One cannot praise the pond-lily; his best words mar it, like the insects that eat its petals: but he can contemplate it as it opens in the morning sun and distills such perfume, such purity, such snow of petal and such gold of anther, from the dark water and still darker ooze. How feminine it seems beside its coarser and more robust congeners; how shy, how pliant, how fine in texture and star-like in form!

The loosestrife is a foreign plant, but it has made itself thoroughly at home here, and its masses of royal purple make the woods look civil and festive. The cardinal burns with a more intense fire, and fairly lights up the little dark nooks where it glasses itself in the still water. One must pause and look at it. Its intensity, its pure scarlet, the dark background upon which it is projected, its image in the still darker water, and its general air of retirement and seclusion, all arrest and delight the eye. It is a heart-throb of color on the bosom of the dark solitude.

The rarest and wildest animal that my neighborhood boasts of is the otter. Every winter we see the tracks of one or more

of them upon the snow along Black Creek. But the eye that
has seen the animal itself in recent years I cannot find. It
probably makes its excursions along the creek by night. Follow
its track—as large as that of a fair-sized dog—over the ice,
and you will find that it ends at every open pool and rapid,
and begins again upon the ice beyond. Sometimes it makes
little excursions up the bank, its body often dragging in the
snow like a log. My son followed the track one day far up the
mountain-side, where the absence of the snow caused him to
lose it. I like to think of so wild and shy a creature holding
its own within sound of the locomotive's whistle.

The fox passes my door in winter, and probably in summer
too, as do also the 'possum and the coon. The latter tears
down my sweet corn in the garden, and the rabbit eats off my
raspberry-bushes and nibbles my first strawberries, while the
woodchucks eat my celery and beans and peas. Chipmunks
carry off the corn I put out for the chickens, and weasels eat
the chickens themselves.

Many times during the season I have in my solitude a visit
from a bald eagle. There is a dead tree near the summit, where
he often perches, and which we call the "old eagle-tree." It
is a pine, killed years ago by a thunderbolt,—the bolt of
Jove,—and now the bird of Jove hovers about it or sits upon
it. I have little doubt that what attracted me to this spot attracts
him,—the seclusion, the savageness, the elemental grandeur.
Sometimes, as I look out of my window early in the morning,
I see the eagle upon his perch, preening his plumage, or waiting
for the rising sun to gild the mountain-tops. When the smoke
begins to rise from my chimney, or he sees me going to the
spring for water, he concludes it is time for him to be off. But

he need not fear the crack of the rifle here; nothing more deadly than field-glasses shall be pointed at him while I am about. Often in the course of the day I see him circling above my domain, or winging his way toward the mountains. His home is apparently in the Shawangunk Range, twenty or more miles distant, and I fancy he stops or lingers above me on his way to the river. The days on which I see him are not quite the same as the other days. I think my thoughts soar a little higher all the rest of the morning: I have had a visit from a messenger of Jove. The lift or range of those great wings has passed into my thought. I once heard a collector get up in a scientific body and tell how many eggs of the bald eagle he had clutched that season, how many from this nest, how many from that, and how one of the eagles had deported itself after he had killed its mate. I felt ashamed for him. He had only proved himself a superior human weasel. The man with the rifle and the man with the collector's craze are fast reducing the number of eagles in the country. Twenty years ago I used to see a dozen or more along the river in the spring when the ice was breaking up, where I now see only one or two, or none at all. In the present case, what would it profit me could I find and plunder my eagle's nest, or strip his skin from his dead carcass? Should I know him better? I do not want to know him that way. I want rather to feel the inspiration of his presence and noble bearing. I want my interest and sympathy to go with him in his continental voyaging up and down, and in his long, elevated flights to and from his eyrie upon the remote, solitary cliffs. He draws great lines across the sky; he sees the forests like a carpet beneath him, he sees the hills and valleys as folds and wrinkles in a many-colored tapestry; he sees the river as a silver belt connecting remote horizons. We climb mountain-peaks to get a glimpse of the spectacle that is hourly spread out beneath him. Dignity, elevation, repose, are his. I would have my thoughts take as wide a sweep. I would be as far removed from the petty cares and turmoils of this noisy and blustering world.

THE ART OF
SEEING THINGS

I

I do not purpose to attempt to tell my reader how to see things, but only to talk about the art of seeing things, as one might talk of any other art. One might discourse about the art of poetry, or of painting, or of oratory, without any hope of making one's readers or hearers poets or painters or orators.

The science of anything may be taught or acquired by study; the art of it comes by practice or inspiration. The art of seeing things is not something that may be conveyed in rules and precepts; it is a matter vital in the eye and ear, yea, in the mind and soul, of which these are the organs. I have as little hope of being able to tell the reader how to see things as I would have in trying to tell him how to fall in love or to enjoy his dinner. Either he does or he does not, and that is about all there is of it. Some people seem born with eyes in their heads, and others with buttons or painted marbles, and no amount of science can make the one equal to the other in the art of seeing things. The great mass of mankind are, in this respect, like the rank and file of an army: they fire vaguely in the direction of the enemy, and if they hit, it is more a matter of chance than of accurate aim. But here and there is the keen-eyed observer; he is the sharpshooter; his eye selects and discriminates, his purpose goes to the mark.

Even the successful angler seems born, and not made; he appears to know instinctively the ways of trout. The secret is, no doubt, love of the sport. Love sharpens the eye, the ear, the touch; it quickens the feet, it steadies the hand, it arms against the wet and the cold. What we love to do, that we do well. To know is not all; it is only half. To love is the other half. Wordsworth's poet was contented if he might enjoy the things which others understood. This is generally the attitude of the young and of the poetic nature. The man of science, on the other hand, is contented if he may understand the things that others enjoy: that is his enjoyment. Contemplation and absorption for the one; investigation and classification for the other. We probably all have, in varying degrees, one or the other of these ways of enjoying Nature: either the sympathetic and emotional enjoyment of her which the young and the artistic and the poetic temperament have, or the enjoyment through our knowing faculties afforded by natural science, or, it may be, the two combined, as they certainly were in such a man as Tyndall.

But nothing can take the place of love. Love is the measure of life: only so far as we love do we really live. The variety of our interests, the width of our sympathies, the susceptibilities of our hearts—if these do not measure our lives, what does? As the years go by, we are all of us more or less subject to two dangers, the danger of petrifaction and the danger of putrefaction; either that we shall become hard and callous, crusted over with customs and conventions till no new ray of light or of joy can reach us, or that we shall become lax and disorganized, losing our grip upon the real and vital sources of happiness and power. Now, there is no preservative and antiseptic, nothing that keeps one's heart young, like love, like sympathy, like giving one's self with enthusiasm to some worthy thing or cause.

If I were to name the three most precious resources of life, I should say books, friends, and nature; and the greatest of these, at least the most constant and always at hand, is nature. Nature we have always with us, an inexhaustible storehouse of that which moves the heart, appeals to the mind, and fires the imagination,—health to the body, a stimulus to the intellect, and joy to the soul. To the scientist Nature is a storehouse of facts, laws, processes; to the artist she is a storehouse of pictures; to the poet she is a storehouse of images, fancies, a source of inspiration; to the moralist she is a storehouse of precepts and parables; to all she may be a source of knowledge and joy.

II

There is nothing in which people differ more than in their powers of observation. Some are only half alive to what is going on around them. Others, again, are keenly alive: their intelligence, their powers of recognition, are in full force in eye and ear at all times. They see and hear everything, whether it directly concerns them or not. They never pass unseen a familiar face on the street; they are never oblivious of any interesting feature or sound or object in the earth or sky about them. Their power of attention is always on the alert, not by conscious effort, but by natural habit and disposition. Their perceptive faculties may be said to be always on duty. They turn to the outward world a more highly sensitized mind than other people. The things that pass before them are caught and individualized instantly. If they visit new countries, they see the characteristic features of the people and scenery at once. The impression is never blurred or confused. Their powers of observation suggest the sight and scent of wild animals; only, whereas it is fear that sharpens the one, it is love and curiosity that sharpens the other. The mother turkey with her brood sees the hawk when it is a mere speck against the sky; she is, in her solicitude for her young, thinking of hawks, and is on her guard against them. Fear makes keen her eye. The hunter does not see the hawk till his attention is thus called to it by the turkey, because his interests are not endangered; but he out-sees the wild creatures of the plain and mountain,—the elk, the antelope, and the mountain-sheep,—he makes it his busi-ness to look for them, and his eyes carry farther than do theirs.

We may see coarsely and vaguely, as most people do, noting only masses and unusual appearances, or we may see finely and discriminatingly, taking in the minute and the spe-cific. In a collection of stuffed birds, the other day, I observed that a wood thrush was mounted as in the act of song, its open beak pointing straight to the zenith. The taxidermist had not seen truly. The thrush sings with its beak but slightly elevated. Who has not seen a red squirrel or a gray squirrel running up and down the trunk of a tree? But probably very few have noticed that the position of the hind feet is the reverse in the one case from what it is in the other. In descending they are extended to the rear, the toe-nails hooking to the bark, check-ing and controlling the fall. In most pictures the feet are shown well drawn up under the body in both cases.

People who discourse pleasantly and accurately about the

birds and flowers and external nature generally are not invariably good observers. In their walks do they see anything they did not come out to see? Is there any spontaneous or unpremeditated seeing? Do they make discoveries? Any bird or creature may be hunted down, any nest discovered, if you lay siege to it; but to find what you are not looking for, to catch the shy winks and gestures on every side, to see all the by-play going on around you, missing no significant note or movement, penetrating every screen with your eye-beams—that is to be an observer; that is to have "an eye practiced like a blind man's touch,"—a touch that can distinguish a white horse from a black,—a detective eye that reads the faintest signs. When Thoreau was at Cape Cod, he noticed that the horses there had a certain muscle in their hips inordinately developed by reason of the insecure footing in the ever-yielding sand. Thoreau's vision at times fitted things closely. During some great fête in Paris, the Empress Eugénie and Queen Victoria were both present. A reporter noticed that when the royal personages came to sit down, Eugénie looked behind her before doing so, to see that the chair was really there, but Victoria seated herself without the backward glance, knowing there must be a seat ready: there always had been, and there always would be, for her. The correspondent inferred that the incident showed the difference between born royalty and hastily made royalty. I wonder how many persons in that vast assembly made this observation; probably very few. It denoted a gift for seeing things.

If our powers of observation were quick and sure enough, no doubt we should see through most of the tricks of the sleight-of-hand man. He fools us because his hand is more dexterous than our eye. He captures our attention, and then commands us to see only what he wishes us to see.

In the field of natural history, things escape us because the actors are small, and the stage is very large and more or less veiled and obstructed. The movement is quick across a background that tends to conceal rather than expose it. In the printed page the white paper plays quite as important a part as the type and the ink; but the book of nature is on a different plan: the page rarely presents a contrast of black and white, or even black and brown, but only of similar tints, gray upon gray, green upon green, or drab upon brown.

By a close observer I do not mean a minute, cold-blooded specialist,—

> "a fingering slave,
> One who would peep and botanize
> Upon his mother's grave."—

but a man who looks closely and steadily at nature, and notes the individual features of tree and rock and field, and allows no subtle flavor of the night or day, of the place and the season, to escape him. His senses are so delicate that in his evening walk he feels the warm and the cool streaks in the air, his nose detects the most fugitive odors, his ears the most furtive sounds. As he stands musing in the April twilight, he hears that fine, elusive stir and rustle made by the angleworms reaching out from their holes for leaves and grasses; he hears the whistling wings of the woodcock as it goes swiftly by him in the dusk; he hears the call of the killdee come down out of the March sky; he hears far above him in the early morning the squeaking cackle of the arriving blackbirds pushing north;

he hears the soft, prolonged, lulling call of the little owl in the cedars in the early spring twilight; he hears at night the roar of the distant waterfall, and the rumble of the train miles across the country when the air is "hollow"; before a storm he notes how distant objects stand out and are brought near on those brilliant days that we call "weather-breeders." When the mercury is at zero or lower, he notes how the passing trains hiss and simmer as if the rails or wheels were red-hot. He reads the subtile signs of the weather. The stars at night forecast the coming day to him; the clouds at evening and at morning are a sign. He knows there is the wet-weather diathesis and the dry-weather diathesis, or, as Goethe said, water affirmative and water negative, and he interprets the symptoms accordingly. He is keenly alive to all outward impressions. When he descends from the hill in the autumn twilight, he notes the cooler air of the valley like a lake about him; he notes how, at other seasons, the cooler air at times settles down between the mountains like a vast body of water, as shown by the level line of the fog or the frost upon the trees.

The modern man looks at nature with an eye of sympathy and love where the earlier man looked with an eye of fear and superstition. Hence he sees more closely and accurately; science has made his eye steady and clear. To a hasty traveler through the land, the farms and country homes all seem much alike, but to the people born and reared there, what a difference! They have read the fine print that escapes the hurried eye and that is so full of meaning. Every horizon line, every curve in hill or valley, every tree and rock and spring run, every turn in the road and vista in the landscape, has its special features and makes its own impression.

Scott wrote in his journal: "Nothing is so tiresome as walking through some beautiful scene with a minute philosopher, a botanist, or a pebble-gatherer, who is eternally calling your attention from the grand features of the natural picture to look at grasses and chuckie-stanes." No doubt Scott's large, generous way of looking at things kindles the imagination and touches the sentiments more than does this minute way of the specialist. The nature that Scott gives us is like the air and the water that all may absorb, while what the specialist gives us is more like some particular element or substance that only the few can appropriate. But Scott had his specialties, too, the specialties of the sportsman: he was the first to see the hare's eyes as she sat in her form, and he knew the ways of grouse and pheasants and trout. The ideal observer turns the enthusiasm of the sportsman into the channels of natural history, and brings home a finer game than ever fell to shot or bullet. He too has an eye for the fox and the rabbit and the migrating water-fowl, but he sees them with loving and not with murderous eyes.

III

So far as seeing things is an art, it is the art of keeping your eyes and ears open. The art of nature is all in the direction of concealment. The birds, the animals, all the wild creatures, for the most part try to elude your observation. The art of the bird is to hide her nest; the art of the game you are in quest of is to make itself invisible. The flower seeks to attract the bee and the moth by its color and perfume, because they are of service to it; but I presume it would hide from the excursionists and the picnickers if it could, because they extirpate it. Power of attention and a mind sensitive to outward objects, in these lies the secret of seeing things. Can you bring all your faculties to the front, like a house with many faces at the doors and windows; or do you live retired within yourself, shut up in your own meditations? The thinker puts all the powers of his mind in reflection: the observer puts all the powers of his mind in perception; every faculty is directed outward; the whole mind sees through the eye and hears through the ear. He has an objective turn of mind as opposed to a subjective. A person with the latter turn of mind sees little. If you are occupied with your own thoughts, you may go through a museum of curiosities and observe nothing.

Of course one's powers of observation may be cultivated as well as anything else. The senses of seeing and hearing may be quickened and trained as well as the sense of touch. Blind persons come to be marvelously acute in their powers of touch. Their feet find the path and keep it. They come to know the lay of the land through this sense, and recognize the roads and surfaces they have once traveled over. Helen Keller reads your speech by putting her hand upon your lips, and is thrilled by the music of an instrument through the same sense of touch. The perceptions of school-children should be trained as well as their powers of reflection and memory. A teacher in Connecticut, Miss Aiken,—whose work on mind-training I commend to all teachers,—has hit upon a simple and ingenious method of doing this. She has a revolving blackboard upon which she writes various figures, numbers, words, sentences, which she exposes to the view of the class for one or two or three seconds, as the case may be, and then asks them to copy or repeat what was written. In time they become astonishingly quick, especially the girls, and can take in a multitude of things at a glance. Detectives, I am told, are trained after a similar method; a man is led quickly by a show-window, for instance, and asked to name and describe the objects he saw there. Life itself is of course more or less a school of this kind, but the power of concentrated attention in most persons needs stimulating. Here comes in the benefit of manual-training schools. To *do* a thing, to make something, the powers of the mind must be focused. A boy in building a boat will get something that all the books in the world cannot give him. The concrete, the definite, the discipline of real things, the educational values that lie here, are not enough appreciated.

IV

The book of nature is like a page written over or printed upon with different-sized characters and in many different languages, interlined and crosslined, and with a great variety of marginal notes and references. There is coarse print and fine print; there are obscure signs and hieroglyphics. We all read the large type more or less appreciatively, but only the students and lovers of nature read the fine lines and the footnotes. It is a book which he reads best who goes most slowly or even tarries long by the way. He who runs may read some things. We may take in the general features of sky, plain, and river from the express train, but only the pedestrian, the saunterer, with eyes in his head and love in his heart, turns every leaf and peruses every line. One man sees only the migrating waterfowls and the larger birds of the air; another sees the passing kinglets and hurrying warblers as well. For my part, my delight is to linger long over each page of this marvelous record, and to dwell fondly upon its most obscure text.

I take pleasure in noting the minute things about me. I am

interested even in the ways of the wild bees, and in all the little dramas and tragedies that occur in field and wood. One June day, in my walk, as I crossed a rather dry, high-lying field, my attention was attracted by small mounds of fresh earth all over the ground, scarcely more than a handful in each. On looking closely, I saw that in the middle of each mound there was a hole not quite so large as a lead-pencil. Now, I had never observed these mounds before, and my curiosity was aroused. "Here is some fine print," I said, "that I have over-looked." So I set to work to try to read it; I waited for a sign of life. Presently I saw here and there a bee hovering about over the mounds. It looked like the honey-bee, only less pronounced in color and manner. One of them alighted on one of the mounds near me, and was about to disappear in the hole in the centre when I caught it in my hand. Though it stung me, I retained it and looked it over, and in the process was stung several times; but the pain was slight. I saw it was one of our native wild bees, cousin to the leaf-rollers, that build their nests under stones and in decayed fence-rails. (In Packard I found it described under the name of *Andrena*.) Then I inserted a small weed-stalk into one of the holes, and, with a little trowel I carried, proceeded to dig out the nest. The hole was about a foot deep; at the bottom of it I found a little semi-transparent, membranous sac or cell, a little larger than that of the honey-bee; in this sac was a little pellet of yellow pollen—a loaf of bread for the young grub when the egg should have hatched. I explored other nests and found them all the same. This discovery was not a great addition to my sum of natural knowledge, but it was something. Now when I see the signs in a field, I know what they mean: they indicate the tiny earthen cradles of *Andrena*.

Near by I chanced to spy a large hole in the turf, with no mound of soil about it. I could put the end of my little finger into it. I peered down, and saw the gleam of two small, bead-like eyes. I knew it to be the den of the wolf-spider. Was she waiting for some blundering insect to tumble in? I say she, because the real ogre among the spiders is the female. The male is small and of little consequence. A few days later I paused by this den again and saw the members of the ogress scattered about her own door. Had some insect Jack the Giant-Killer been there, or had a still more formidable ogress, the sand-hornet, dragged her forth and carried away her limbless body to her den in the bank?

What the wolf-spider does with the earth it excavates in making its den is a mystery. There is no sign of it anywhere about. Does it force its way down by pushing the soil to one side and packing it there firmly? The entrance to the hole usually has a slight rim or hem to keep the edge from crumbling in.

As it happened, I chanced upon another interesting footnote that very day. I was on my way to a muck swamp in the woods, to see if the showy lady's-slipper was in bloom. Just on the margin of the swamp, in the deep shade of the hemlocks, my eye took note of some small, unshapely creature crawling hurriedly over the ground. I stooped down, and saw it was some large species of moth just out of its case, and in a great hurry to find a suitable place in which to hang itself up and give its wings a chance to unfold before the air dried them. I thrust a small twig in its way, which it instantly seized upon. I lifted it gently, carried it to drier ground, and fixed the stick in the fork of a tree, so that the moth hung free a few feet from the ground. Its body was distended nearly to the size of one's little

finger, and surmounted by wings that were so crumpled and
stubby that they seemed quite rudimentary. The creature evidently knew what it wanted, and knew the importance of haste.
Instantly these rude, stubby wings began to grow. It was a slow
process, but one could see the change from minute to minute.
As the wings expanded, the body contracted. By some kind of
pumping arrangement air was being forced from a reservoir in
the one into the tubes of the other. The wings were not really
growing, as they at first seemed to be, but they were unfolding
and expanding under this pneumatic pressure from the body.
In the course of about half an hour the process was completed,
and the winged creature hung there in all its full-fledged
beauty. Its color was checked black and white like a loon's
back, but its name I know not. My chief interest in it, aside
from the interest we feel in any new form of life, arose from
the creature's extreme anxiety to reach a perch where it could
unfold its wings. A little delay would doubtless have been fatal
to it. I wonder how many human geniuses are hatched whose
wings are blighted by some accident or untoward circumstance.
Or do the wings of genius always unfold, no matter what the
environment may be?

One seldom takes a walk without encountering some of this
fine print on nature's page. Now it is a little yellowish-white
moth that spreads itself upon the middle of a leaf as if to imitate
the droppings of birds; or it is the young cicadas working up
out of the ground, and in the damp, cool places building little
chimneys or tubes above the surface to get more warmth and
hasten their development; or it is a wood-newt gorging a tree-
cricket, or a small snake gorging the newt, or a bird song with
some striking peculiarity—a strange defect, or a rare excel-
lence. Now it is a shrike impaling his victim, or blue jays

mocking and teasing a hawk and dropping quickly into the branches to avoid his angry blows, or a robin hustling a cuckoo out of the tree where her nest is, or a vireo driving away a cowbird, or the partridge blustering about your feet till her young are hidden. One October morning I was walking along the road on the edge of the woods, when I came into a gentle shower of butternuts; one of them struck my hat-brim. I paused and looked about me; here one fell, there another, yonder a third. There was no wind blowing, and I wondered what was loosening the butternuts. Turning my attention to the top of the tree, I soon saw the explanation: a red squirrel was at work gathering his harvest. He would seize a nut, give it a twist, when down it would come; then he would dart to another and another. Farther along I found where he had covered the ground with chestnut burs; he could not wait for the frost and the winds; did he know that the burs would dry and open upon the ground, and that the bitter covering of the butternuts would soon fall away from the nut?

There are three things that perhaps happen near me each season that I have never yet seen—the toad casting its skin, the snake swallowing its young, and the larvæ of the moth and butterfly constructing their shrouds. It is a mooted question whether or not the snake does swallow its young, but if there is no other good reason for it, may they not retreat into their mother's stomach to feed? How else are they to be nourished? That the moth larva can weave its own cocoon and attach it to a twig seems more incredible. Yesterday, in my walk, I found a firm, silver-gray cocoon, about two inches long and shaped like an Egyptian mummy (probably *Promethea*), suspended from a branch of a bush by a narrow, stout ribbon twice as long as itself. The fastening was woven around the limb, upon which it turned as if it grew there. I would have given something to have seen the creature perform this feat, and then incase itself so snugly in the silken shroud at the end of this tether. By swinging free, its firm, compact case was in no danger from woodpeckers, as it might have been if resting directly upon a branch or tree-trunk. Near by was the cocoon of another species (*Cecropia*) that was fastened directly to the limb; but this was vague, loose, and much more involved and net-like. I have seen the downy woodpecker assaulting one of these cocoons, but its yielding surface and webby interior seemed to puzzle and baffle him.

I am interested even in the way each climbing plant or vine goes up the pole, whether from right to left, or from left to right,—that is, with the hands of a clock or against them, —whether it is under the law of the great cyclonic storms of the northern hemisphere, which all move against the hands of a clock, or in the contrary direction, like the cyclones in the southern hemisphere. I take pleasure in noting every little dancing whirlwind of a summer day that catches up the dust or the leaves before me, and every little funnel-shaped whirl-pool in the swollen stream or river, whether or not they spin from right to left or the reverse. If I were in the southern hemisphere, I am sure I should note whether these things were under the law of its cyclones in this respect or under the law of ours. As a rule, our twining plants and toy whirlwinds copy our revolving storms and go against the hands of the clock. But there are exceptions. While the bean, the bittersweet, the morning-glory, and others go up from left to right, the hop, the wild buckwheat, and some others go up from right to left. Most of our forest trees show a tendency to wind one way or the other, the hard woods going in one direction, and the hemlocks and pines and cedars and butternuts and chestnuts in another. In different localities, or on different geological formations, I find these directions reversed. I recall one instance in the case of a hemlock six or seven inches in diameter, where this tendency to twist had come out of the grain, as it were, and shaped the outward form of the tree, causing it to make, in an ascent of about thirty feet, one complete revolution about a larger tree close to which it grew. On a smaller scale I have seen the same thing in a pine.

Persons lost in the woods or on the plains, or traveling at night, tend, I believe, toward the left. The movements of men and women, it is said, differ in this respect, one sex turning to the right and the other to the left.

I had lived in the world more than fifty years before I noticed a peculiarity about the rays of light one often sees diverging from an opening, or a series of openings, in the clouds, namely, that they are like spokes in a wheel, the hub, or centre, of which appears to be just there in the vapory masses, instead of being, as is really the case, nearly ninety-three millions of miles beyond. The beams of light that come through cracks or chinks in a wall do not converge in this way, but to the eye run parallel to one another. There is another fact: this fan-shaped display of converging rays is always immediately in front of the observer; that is, exactly between him and the sun, so that the central spoke or shaft in his front is always perpendicular. You cannot see this fan to the right or left of the sun, but only between you and it. Hence, as in the case of the rainbow, no two persons see exactly the same rays.

The eye sees what it has the means of seeing, and its means of seeing are in proportion to the love and desire behind it. The eye is informed and sharpened by the thought. My boy sees ducks on the river where and when I cannot, because at certain seasons he thinks ducks and dreams ducks. One season my neighbor asked me if the bees had injured my grapes. I said, "No; the bees never injure my grapes."

"They do mine," he replied; "they puncture the skin for the juice, and at times the clusters are covered with them."

"No," I said, "it is not the bees that puncture the skin; it is the birds."

"What birds?"

"The orioles."

"But I haven't seen any orioles," he rejoined.

"We have," I continued, "because at this season we think orioles; we have learned by experience how destructive these birds are in the vineyard, and we are on the lookout for them; our eyes and ears are ready for them."

If we think birds, we shall see birds wherever we go; if we think arrowheads, as Thoreau did, we shall pick up arrowheads in every field. Some people have an eye for four-leaved clovers; they see them as they walk hastily over the turf, for they already have them in their eyes. I once took a walk with the late Professor Eaton of Yale. He was just then specially interested in the mosses, and he found them, all kinds, everywhere. I can see him yet, every few minutes upon his knees, adjusting his eye-glasses before some rare specimen. The beauty he found in them, and pointed out to me, kindled my enthusiasm also. I once spent a summer day at the mountain home of a well-known literary woman and editor. She lamented the absence of birds about her house. I named a half-dozen or more I had heard or seen in her trees within an hour—the indigo-bird, the purple finch, the yellowbird, the veery thrush, the red-eyed vireo, the song sparrow.

"Do you mean to say you have seen or heard all these birds while sitting here on my porch?" she inquired.

"I really have," I said.

"I do not see them or hear them," she replied, "and yet I want to very much."

"No," said I; "you only *want to want* to see and hear them."

You must have the bird in your heart before you can find it in the bush.

I was sitting in front of a farmhouse one day in company with the local Nimrod. In a maple tree in front of us I saw the great crested flycatcher. I called the hunter's attention to it, and asked him if he had ever seen that bird before. No, he had not; it was a new bird to him. But he probably had seen it scores of times,—seen it without regarding it. It was not the game he was in quest of, and his eye heeded it not.

Human and artificial sounds and objects thrust themselves upon us; they are within our sphere, so to speak: but the life of nature we must meet halfway; it is shy, withdrawn, and blends itself with a vast neutral background. We must be initiated; it is an order the secrets of which are well guarded.

A WALK IN
THE FIELDS

Let us go and walk in the fields. It is the middle of a very early March—a March that has in some way cut out April and got into its place.

I knew an Irish laborer, who during his last illness thought, when spring came, if he could walk in the fields, he would get well. I have observed that farmers, when harassed by trouble, or weighed down by grief, are often wont to go and walk alone in the fields. They find dumb sympathy and companionship there. I knew a farmer who, after the death of his only son, would frequently get up in the middle of the night and go and walk in his fields. It was said that he had been harsh and unjust to his son, and, during the last day the latter had worked and when the fatal illness was coming upon him, the father had severely upbraided him because he left his task and sat for a while under the fence. One can fancy him going to this very spot in his midnight wanderings, and standing in mute agony where the cruel words had been spoken, or throwing himself upon the ground, pleading in vain at the door of the irrevocable past. That door never opens again, plead you there till your heart breaks.

A farmer's fields become in time almost a part of himself: his life history is written all over them; virtue has gone out of himself into them; he has fertilized them with the sweat of his brow; he knows the look and the quality of each one. This one he reclaimed from the wilderness when he came on the farm as a young man; he sowed rye among the stumps and scratched it in with a thorn brush; as the years went by he saw the stumps slowly decay; he would send his boys to set fire to them in the dry spring weather;—I was one of those boys, and it seems as if I could smell the pungent odor of those burning stumps at this moment: now this field is one of his smoothest, finest meadows. This one was once a rough pasture; he pried up or blasted out the rocks, and with his oxen drew them into a line along the border of the woods, and with stone picked or dug from the surface built upon them a solid four-foot wall; now the mowing-machine runs evenly where once the cattle grazed with difficulty.

I was a boy when that field was cleaned up. I took a hand —a boy's hand—in the work. I helped pick up the loose stone, which we drew upon a stone-boat shod with green poles. It was back-aching work, and it soon wore the skin thin on the ends of the fingers. How the crickets and ants and beetles would rush about when we uncovered them! They no doubt looked upon the stone that sheltered them as an old institution that we had no right to remove. No right, my little folk, only the might of the stronger. Sometimes a flat stone would prove the roof of a mouse-nest—a blinking, bead-eyed, meadow-mouse. What consternation would seize him, too, as he would rush off along the little round beaten ways under the dry grass and weeds! Many of the large bowlders were deeply imbedded in the soil, and only stuck their noses or heads, so to speak, up through the turf. These we would first tackle with the big lever, a long, dry, ironwood pole, as heavy as one could handle, shod with a horseshoe. With the end of this thrust under the end or edge of a bowlder, and resting upon a stone for a fulcrum, we would begin the assault. Inch by inch the turf-bound rock would yield. Sometimes the lever would slip its hold, and come down upon our heads if we were not watchful. As the rock yielded, the lever required more bait, as the farmer calls it, —an addition to the fulcrum. After the rock was raised sufficiently, we would prop it up with stones, arrange a skid or skids under it—green beech poles cut in the woods—wrap a chain around it, and hitch the oxen to it, directing them to the right or left to turn the bowlder out of its bed and place it on the surface of the ground. When this was accomplished, then came the dead straight pull to the line of the fence. An old, experienced ox-team know what is before them, or rather behind them; they have felt the bowlder and sized it up. At the word and the crack of the whip they bend their heads and throw their weight upon the yoke. Now the hickory bows settle into their shoulders, they kink their tails and hump their backs, their sharp hoofs cut the turf, and the great inert mass moves. Tearing up the sod, grinding over stones, the shouts of the excited driver urging them on, away they go toward the line. The peculiar and agreeable odor of burnt and ground stone arises from the rear. Only a few yards at a time; how the oxen puff as they halt to take breath and lap their tongues out over their moist muzzles! Then they bend to the work again, the muscular effort reaching their very tails. Thus the work goes on for several days or a week, till the row of bottom rocks is complete. If there are others remaining in the field, then the row is doubled up till the land is cleaned.

What a torn and wounded appearance that section of ground presents, its surface everywhere marked with red stripes or bands, each ending in or starting from a large and deep red cavity in the sward! But soon the plow will come, equalizing and obliterating and writing another history upon the page.

There is something to me peculiarly interesting in stone walls—a kind of rude human expression to them, suggesting the face of the old farmer himself. How they climb the hills and sweep through the valleys. They decay not, yet they grow old and decrepit; little by little they lose their precision and firmness, they stagger, then fall. In a still, early spring morning or April twilight one often hears a rattle of stones in a distant field; some bit of old wall is falling. The lifetime of the best of them is rarely threescore and ten. The other day, along the highway, I saw an old man relaying a dilapidated stone wall. "Fifty-three years ago," he said, "I laid this wall. When it is laid again, I shan't have the job." It is rarely now that one sees a new wall going up. The fences have all been built, and the farmer has only to keep them in repair.

When you build a field or a highway wall, do not make the top of it level across the little hollows; let it bend to the uneven surface, let it look flexible and alive. A foundation wall, with its horizontal lines, looks stiff and formal, but a wall that undulates along like a live thing pleases the eye.

When I was a boy upon the old farm, my father always "laid out" to build forty or fifty rods of new wall, or rebuild as many rods of old wall, each spring. It is true husbandry to fence your field with the stones that incumber it, to utilize obstacles. The walls upon the old farm of which I am thinking have each a history. This one, along the lower side of the road, was built in '46. I remember the man who laid it. I even remember something of the complexion of the May days when the work was going on. It was built from a still older wall, and new material added. It leans and staggers in places now like an old man, but it is still a substantial fence. This one upon the upper side of the road, my father told me he built the year he came upon the farm, which was in '28. He paid twenty cents a rod for having it laid to a man whose grandchildren are now gray-haired men. The wall has a rock foundation, and it still holds its course without much wavering.

The more padding there is in a stone wall, the less enduring it is. Let your stone reach clean through. A smooth face will not save it; a loose and cobbly interior will be its ruin. Let there be a broad foundation, let the parts be well bound together, let the joints be carefully broken, and, above all, let its height not be too great for its width. If it is too high, it will topple over; if its interior is defective, it will spread and collapse. Time searches out its every weakness, and respects only good material and good workmanship.

A HUNT FOR THE
NIGHTINGALE

While I lingered away the latter half of May in Scotland, and the first half of June in northern England, and finally in London, intent on seeing the land leisurely and as the mood suited, the thought never occurred to me that I was in danger of missing one of the chief pleasures I had promised myself in crossing the Atlantic, namely, the hearing of the song of the nightingale. Hence, when on the 17th of June I found myself down among the copses near Hazlemere, on the borders of Surrey and Sussex, and was told by the old farmer, to whose house I had been recommended by friends in London, that I was too late, that the season of the nightingale was over, I was a good deal disturbed.

"I think she be done singing now, sir; I ain't heered her in some time, sir," said my farmer, as we sat down to get acquainted over a mug of the hardest cider I ever attempted to drink.

"Too late!" I said in deep chagrin, "and I might have been here weeks ago."

"Yeas, sir, she be done now; May is the time to hear her.

The cuckoo is done too, sir; and you don't hear the nightingale after the cuckoo is gone, sir."

(The country people in this part of England *sir* one at the end of every sentence, and talk with an indescribable drawl.)

But I had heard a cuckoo that very afternoon, and I took heart from the fact. I afterward learned that the country people everywhere associate these two birds in this way; you will not hear the one after the other has ceased. But I heard the cuckoo almost daily till the middle of July. Matthew Arnold reflects the popular opinion when in one of his poems ("Thyrsis") he makes the cuckoo say in early June,—

"The bloom is gone, and with the bloom go I!"

The explanation is to be found in Shakespeare, who says,—

"The cuckoo is in June
Heard, not regarded,"

as the bird really does not go till August. I got out my Gilbert White, as I should have done at an earlier day, and was still more disturbed to find that he limited the singing of the nightingale to June 15. But seasons differ, I thought, and it can't be possible that any class of feathered songsters all stop on a given day. There is a tradition that when George I. died the nightingales all ceased singing for the year out of grief at the sad event; but his majesty did not die till June 21. This would give me a margin of several days. Then, when I looked further in White, and found that he says the chaffinch ceases to sing the beginning of June, I took more courage, for I had that day heard the chaffinch also. But it was evident I had no time to lose; I was just on the dividing line, and any day might witness the cessation of the last songster. For it seems that the nightingale ceases singing the moment her brood is hatched. After that event, you hear only a harsh chiding or anxious note. Hence the poets, who attribute her melancholy strains to sorrow for the loss of her young, are entirely at fault. Virgil, portraying the grief of Orpheus after the loss of Eurydice, says:—

> "So Philomela, 'mid the poplar shade,
> Bemoans her captive brood; the cruel hind
> Saw them unplumed, and took them; but all night
> Grieves she, and, sitting on a bough, runs o'er
> Her wretched tale, and fills the woods with woe."

But she probably does nothing of the kind. The song of a bird is not a reminiscence, but an anticipation, and expresses happiness or joy only, except in those cases where the male bird, having lost its mate, sings for a few days as if to call the lost one back. When the male renews his powers of song, after the young brood has been destroyed, or after it has flown away, it is a sign that a new brood is contemplated. The song is, as it were, the magic note that calls the brood forth. At least, this is the habit with other song-birds, and I have no doubt the same holds good with the nightingale. Destroy the nest or brood of the wood thrush, and if the season is not too far advanced, after a week or ten days of silence, during which the parent birds by their manner seem to bemoan their loss and to take counsel together, the male breaks forth with a new song, and the female begins to construct a new nest. The poets, therefore, in depicting the bird on such occasions as bewailing the lost brood, are wide of the mark; he is invoking and celebrating a new brood.

As it was mid-afternoon, I could only compose myself till nightfall. I accompanied the farmer to the hay-field and saw the working of his mowing-machine, a rare implement in England, as most of the grass is still cut by hand, and raked by hand also. The disturbed skylarks were hovering above the falling grass, full of anxiety for their nests, as one may note the bobolinks on like occasions at home. The weather is so uncertain in England, and it is so impossible to predict its complexion, not only from day to day but from hour to hour, that the farmers appear to consider it a suitable time to cut grass when it is not actually raining. They slash away without reference to the aspects of the sky, and when the field is down trust to luck to be able to cure the hay, or get it ready to "carry" between the showers. The clouds were lowering and the air was damp now, and it was Saturday afternoon; but the farmer said they would never get their hay if they minded such things. The farm had seen better days; so had the farmer; both were slightly down at the heel. Too high rent and too much hard cider were working their effects upon both. The farm had been in the family many generations, but it was now about to be sold and to pass into other hands, and my host said he was glad of it. There was no money in farming any more; no money in anything. I asked him what were the main sources of profit on such a farm.

"Well," he said, "sometimes the wheat pops up, and the barley drops in, and the pigs come on, and we picks up a little money, sir, but not much, sir. Pigs is doing well naow. But they brings so much wheat from Ameriky, and our weather is so bad that we can't get a good sample, sir, one year in three, that there is no money made in growing wheat, sir." And the "wuts" (oats) were not much better. "Theys as would buy hain't got no money, sir." "Up to the top of the nip," for top of the hill, was one of his expressions. Tennyson had a summer residence at Blackdown, not far off. "One of the Queen's poets, I believe, sir." "Yes, I often see him riding about, sir."

After an hour or two with the farmer, I walked out to take a survey of the surrounding country. It was quite wild and irregular, full of bushy fields and overgrown hedge-rows, and looked to me very nightingaly. I followed for a mile or two a road that led by tangled groves and woods and copses, with a still meadow trout stream in the gentle valley below. I inquired for nightingales of every boy and laboring-man I met or saw. I got but little encouragement; it was too late. "She be about done singing now, sir." A boy whom I met in a footpath that ran through a pasture beside a copse said, after reflecting a moment, that he had heard one in that very copse two mornings before,—"about seven o'clock, sir, while I was on my way to my work, sir." Then I would try my luck in said copse and in the adjoining thickets that night and the next morning. The railway ran near, but perhaps that might serve to keep the birds awake. These copses in this part of England look strange enough to American eyes. What thriftless farming! the first thought is; behold the fields grown up to bushes, as if the land had relapsed to a state of nature again. Adjoining meadows and grain-fields, one may see an inclosure of many acres covered with a thick growth of oak and chestnut sprouts, six or eight or twelve feet high. These are the copses one has so often heard about, and they are a valuable and productive part of the farm. They are planted and preserved as carefully as we plant an orchard or a vineyard. Once in so many years, perhaps five or six, the copse is cut and every twig is saved; it is a woodland harvest that in our own country is gathered in the forest itself. The larger poles are tied up in bundles and sold for hoop-poles; the fine branches and shoots are made into brooms in the neighboring cottages and hamlets, or used as material for thatching. The refuse is used as wood.

About eight o'clock in the evening I sallied forth, taking my way over the ground I had explored a few hours before. The gloaming, which at this season lasts till after ten o'clock, dragged its slow length along. Nine o'clock came, and, though my ear was attuned, the songster was tardy. I hovered about the copses and hedge-rows like one meditating some dark deed; I lingered in a grove and about an overgrown garden and a neglected orchard; I sat on stiles and leaned on wickets, mentally speeding the darkness that should bring my singer out. The weather was damp and chilly, and the tryst grew tiresome. I had brought a rubber water-proof, but not an overcoat. Lining the back of the rubber with a newspaper, I wrapped it about me and sat down, determined to lay siege to my bird. A footpath that ran along the fields and bushes on the other side of the little valley showed every few minutes a woman or girl, or boy or laborer, passing along it. A path near me also had its frequent figures moving along in the dusk. In this country people travel in footpaths as much as in highways. The paths give a private, human touch to the landscape that the roads do not. They are sacred to the human foot. They have the sentiment of domesticity, and suggest the way to cottage doors and to simple, primitive times.

Presently a man with a fishing-rod, and capped, coated, and booted for the work, came through the meadow, and began casting for trout in the stream below me. How he gave himself to the work! how oblivious he was of everything but the one matter in hand! I doubt if he was conscious of the train that passed within a few rods of him. Your born angler is like a hound that scents no game but that which he is in pursuit of.

Every sense and faculty were concentrated upon that hovering fly. This man wooed the stream, quivering with pleasure and expectation. Every foot of it he tickled with his decoy. His close was evidently a short one, and he made the most of it. He lingered over every cast, and repeated it again and again. An American angler would have been out of sight down stream long ago. But this fisherman was not going to bolt his preserve; his line should taste every drop of it. His eager, stealthy movements denoted his enjoyment and his absorption. When a trout was caught, it was quickly rapped on the head and slipped into his basket, as if in punishment for its tardiness in jumping. "Be quicker next time, will you?" (British trout, by the way, are not so beautiful as our own. They have more of a domesticated look. They are less brilliantly marked, and have much coarser scales. There is no gold or vermilion in their coloring.)

Presently there arose from a bushy corner of a near field a low, peculiar purring or humming sound, that sent a thrill through me; of course, I thought my bird was inflating her throat. Then the sound increased, and was answered or repeated in various other directions. It had a curious ventriloquial effect. I presently knew it to be the nightjar or goatsucker, a bird that answers to our whip-poor-will. Very soon the sound seemed to be floating all about me,—*Jr-r-r-r-r* or *Chr-r-r-r-r*, slightly suggesting the call of our toads, but more vague as to direction. Then as it grew darker the birds ceased; the fisherman reeled up and left. No sound was now heard,—not even the voice of a solitary frog anywhere. I never heard a frog in England. About eleven o'clock I moved down by a wood, and stood for an hour on a bridge over the railroad. No voice of bird greeted me till the sedge-warbler struck up her curious nocturne in a hedge near by. It was a singular medley of notes, hurried chirps, trills, calls, warbles, snatched from the songs of other birds, with a half-chiding, remonstrating tone or air running through it all. As there was no other sound to be heard, and as the darkness was complete, it had the effect of a very private and whimsical performance,—as if the little bird had secluded herself there, and was giving vent to her emotions in the most copious and vehement manner. I listened till after midnight, and till the rain began to fall, and the vivacious warbler never ceased for a moment. White says that, if it stops, a stone tossed into the bush near it will set it going again. Its voice is not musical; the quality of it is like that of the loquacious English house sparrows; but its song or medley is so persistently animated, and in such contrast to the gloom and the darkness, that the effect is decidedly pleasing.

This and the nightjar were the only nightingales I heard that night. I returned home, a good deal disappointed, but slept upon my arms, as it were, and was out upon the chase again at four o'clock in the morning. This time I passed down a lane by the neglected garden and orchard, where I was told the birds had sung for weeks past; then under the railroad by a cluster of laborers' cottages, and along a road with many copses and bushy fence-corners on either hand, for two miles, but I heard no nightingales. A boy of whom I inquired seemed half frightened, and went into the house without answering.

After a late breakfast I sallied out again, going farther in the same direction, and was overtaken by several showers. I heard many and frequent bird-songs,—the lark, the wren, the thrush, the blackbird, the whitethroat, the greenfinch, and the hoarse, guttural cooing of the wood-pigeons,—but not the note I was in quest of. I passed up a road that was a deep trench in the side of a hill overgrown with low beeches. The roots of the trees formed a network on the side of the bank, as their branches did above. In a framework of roots, within reach of my hand, I spied a wren's nest, a round hole leading to the interior of a large mass of soft green moss, a structure displaying the taste and neatness of the daintiest of bird architects, and the depth and warmth and snugness of the most ingenious mouse habitation. While lingering here, a young countryman came along whom I engaged in conversation. No, he had not heard the nightingale for a few days; but the previous week he had been in camp with the militia near Guildford, and while on picket duty had heard her nearly all night. " 'Don't she sing splendid to-night?' the boys would say." This was tantalizing; Guildford was within easy reach; but the previous week,—that could not be reached. However, he encouraged me by saying he did not think they were done singing yet, as he had often heard them during haying-time. I inquired for the blackcap, but saw he did not know this bird, and thought I referred to a species of tomtit, which also has a black cap. The woodlark I was also on the lookout for, but he did not know this bird either, and during my various rambles in England I found but one person who did. In Scotland it was confounded with the titlark or pipit.

I next met a man and boy, a villager with a stove-pipe hat on,—and, as it turned out, a man of many trades, tailor, barber, painter, etc.,—from Hazlemere. The absorbing inquiry was put to him also. No, not that day, but a few mornings before he had. But he could easily call one out, if there were any about, as he could imitate them. Plucking a spear of grass, he adjusted it behind his teeth and startled me with the shrill, rapid notes he poured forth. I at once recognized its resemblance to the descriptions I had read of the opening part of the nightingale song,—what is called the "challenge." The boy said, and he himself averred, that it was an exact imitation. The *chew, chew, chew,* and some other parts, were very bird-like, and I had no doubt were correct. I was astonished at the strong, piercing quality of the strain. It echoed in the woods and copses about, but, though oft repeated, brought forth no response. With this man I made an engagement to take a walk that evening at eight o'clock along a certain route where he had heard plenty of nightingales but a few days before. He was confident he could call them out; so was I.

In the afternoon, which had gleams of warm sunshine, I made another excursion, less in hopes of hearing my bird than of finding some one who could direct me to the right spot. Once I thought the game was very near. I met a boy who told me he had heard a nightingale only fifteen minutes before, "on Polecat Hill, sir, just this side the Devil's Punch-bowl, sir!" I had heard of his majesty's punch-bowl before, and of the gibbets near it where three murderers were executed nearly a hundred years ago, but Polecat Hill was a new name to me. The combination did not seem a likely place for nightingales, but I walked rapidly thitherward; I heard several warblers, but not Philomel, and was forced to conclude that probably I had crossed the sea to miss my bird by just fifteen minutes. I met many other boys (is there any country where boys do not prowl about in small bands of a Sunday?) and advertised the object of my search freely among them, offering a reward that made their eyes glisten for the bird in song; but nothing ever came of it. In my desperation, I even presented a letter I had brought to the village squire, just as, in company with his wife, he was about to leave his door for church. He turned back, and, hearing my quest, volunteered to take me on a long walk through the wet grass and bushes of his fields and copses, where he knew the birds were wont to sing. "Too late," he said, and so it did appear. He showed me a fine old edition of White's "Selborne," with notes by some editor whose name I have forgotten. This editor had extended White's date of June 15 to July 1, as the time to which the nightingale continues in song, and I felt like thanking him for it, as it gave me renewed hope. The squire thought there was a chance yet; and in case my man with the spear of grass behind his teeth failed me, he gave me a card to an old naturalist and taxidermist at Godalming, a town nine miles above, who, he felt sure, could put me on the right track if anybody could.

At eight o'clock, the sun yet some distance above the horizon, I was at the door of the barber in Hazlemere. He led the way along one of those delightful footpaths with which this country is threaded, extending to a neighboring village several miles distant. It left the street at Hazlemere, cutting through the houses diagonally, as if the brick walls had made way for it, passed between gardens, through wickets, over stiles, across the highway and railroad, through cultivated fields and a gentleman's park, and on toward its destination,—a broad, well-kept path, that seemed to have the same inevitable right of way as a brook. I was told that it was repaired and looked after the same as the highway. Indeed, it was a public way, public to pedestrians only, and no man could stop or turn it aside. We followed it along the side of a steep hill, with copses and groves sweeping down into the valley below us. It was as wild and picturesque a spot as I had seen in England. The foxglove pierced the lower foliage and wild growths everywhere with its tall spires of purple flowers; the wild honeysuckle, with a ranker and coarser fragrance than our cultivated species, was just opening along the hedges. We paused here, and my guide blew his shrill call; he blew it again and again. How it awoke the echoes, and how it awoke all the other songsters! The valley below us and the slope beyond, which before were silent, were soon musical. The chaffinch, the robin, the black-bird, the thrush—the last the loudest and most copious— seemed to vie with each other and with the loud whistler above them. But we listened in vain for the nightingale's note. Twice my guide struck an attitude and said, impressively, "There! I believe I 'erd 'er." But we were obliged to give it up. A shower came on, and after it had passed we moved to another part of the landscape and repeated our call, but got no response, and as darkness set in we returned to the village.

The situation began to look serious. I knew there was a nightingale somewhere whose brood had been delayed from some cause or other, and who was therefore still in song, but I could not get a clew to the spot. I renewed the search late that night, and again the next morning; I inquired of every man and boy I saw.

> "I met many travelers,
>   Who the road had surely kept;
> They saw not my fine revelers,—
>   These had crossed them while they slept;
> Some had heard their fair report,
>   In the country or the court."

I soon learned to distrust young fellows and their girls who had heard nightingales in the gloaming. I knew one's ears could not always be depended upon on such occasions, nor his eyes either. Larks are seen in buntings, and a wren's song entrances like Philomel's. A young couple of whom I inquired in the train, on my way to Godalming, said Yes, they had heard nightingales just a few moments before on their way to the station, and described the spot, so I could find it if I returned that way. They left the train at the same point I did, and walked up the street in advance of me. I had lost sight of them till they beckoned to me from the corner of the street, near the church, where the prospect opens with a view of a near meadow and a stream shaded by pollard willows. "We heard one now, just there," they said, as I came up. They passed on, and I bent my ear eagerly in the direction. Then I walked farther on, following one of those inevitable footpaths to where it cuts diagonally through the cemetery behind the old church, but I heard nothing save a few notes of the thrush. My ear was too critical and exacting. Then I sought out the old naturalist and taxidermist to whom I had a card from the squire. He was a short, stout man, racy both in look and speech, and kindly. He had a fine collection of birds and animals, in which he took great pride. He pointed out the woodlark and the blackcap to me, and told me where he had seen and heard them. He said I was too late for the nightingale, though I might possibly find one yet in song. But he said she grew hoarse late in the season, and did not sing as a few weeks earlier. He thought our cardinal grosbeak, which he called the Virginia nightingale, as fine a whistler as the nightingale herself. He could not go with me that day, but he would send his boy. Summoning the lad, he gave him minute directions where to take me,— over by Easing, around by Shackerford church, etc., a circuit of four or five miles. Leaving the picturesque old town, we took a road over a broad, gentle hill, lined with great trees, —beeches, elms, oaks,—with rich cultivated fields beyond. The air of peaceful and prosperous human occupancy which everywhere pervades this land seemed especially pronounced through all this section. The sentiment of parks and lawns, easy, large, basking, indifferent of admiration, self-sufficing, and full, everywhere prevailed. The road was like the most perfect private carriage-way. Homeliness, in its true sense, is a word that applies to nearly all English country scenes; home-like, redolent of affectionate care and toil, saturated with rural and domestic contentment; beauty without pride, order without stiffness, age without decay. This people love the country, because it would seem as if the country must first have loved them. In a field I saw for the first time a new species of clover, much grown in parts of England as green fodder for horses. The farmers call it trifolium, probably *Trifolium incarnatum*. The head is two or three inches long, and as red as blood. A field of it under the sunlight presents a most brilliant appearance. As we walked along, I got also my first view of the British blue jay,—a slightly larger bird than ours, with a hoarser voice and much duller plumage. Blue, the tint of the sky, is not so common, and is not found in any such perfection among the British birds as among the American. My boy companion was worthy of observation also. He was a curious specimen, ready and officious, but, as one soon found out, full of duplicity. I questioned him about himself. "I helps he, sir; sometimes I shows people about, and sometimes I does errands. I gets three a week, sir, and lunch and tea. I lives with my grandmother, but I calls her mother, sir. The master and the rector they gives me a character, says I am a good, honest boy, and that it is well I went to school in my youth. I am ten, sir. Last year I had the measles, sir, and I thought I should die; but I got hold of a bottle of medicine, and it tasted like honey, and I takes the whole of it, and it made me well, sir. I never lies, sir. It is good to tell the truth." And yet he would slide off into a lie as if the track in that direction was always greased. Indeed, there was a kind of fluent, unctuous, obsequious effrontery in all he said and did. As the day was warm for that climate, he soon grew tired of the chase. At one point we skirted the grounds of a large house, as thickly planted with trees and shrubs as a forest; many birds were singing there, and for a moment my guide made me believe that among them he recognized the notes of the nightingale. Failing in this, he coolly assured me that the swallow that skimmed along the road in front of us was the nightingale! We presently left the highway and took a footpath. It led along the margin of a large plowed field, shut in by rows of noble trees, the soil of which looked as if it might have been a garden of untold generations. Then the path led through a wicket, and down the side of a wooded hill to a large stream and to the hamlet of Easing. A boy fishing said indifferently that he had heard nightingales there that morning. He had caught a little fish which he said was a gudgeon. "Yes," said my companion in response to a remark of mine, "they's little; but you can eat they if they *is* little." Then we went toward Shackerford church. The road, like most roads in the south of England, was a deep trench. The banks on either side rose fifteen feet, covered with ivy, moss, wild flowers, and the roots of trees. England's best defense against an invading foe is her sunken roads. Whole armies might be ambushed in these trenches, while an enemy moving across the open plain would very often find himself plunging headlong into these hidden pitfalls. Indeed, between the subterranean character of the roads in some places and the high-walled or high-hedged character of it in others, the pedestrian about England is shut out from much he would like to see. I used to envy the bicyclists, perched high upon their rolling stilts. But the footpaths escape the barriers, and one need walk nowhere else if he choose.

Around Shackerford church are copses, and large pine and fir woods. The place was full of birds. My guide threw a stone at a small bird which he declared was a nightingale; and though the missile did not come within three yards of it, yet he said he had hit it, and pretended to search for it on the ground. He must needs invent an opportunity for lying. I told him here I had no further use for him, and he turned cheerfully back, with my shilling in his pocket. I spent the afternoon about the woods and copses near Shackerford. The day was bright and the air balmy. I heard the cuckoo call, and the chaffinch sing, both of which I considered good omens. The little chiffchaff was chiffchaffing in the pine woods. The whitethroat, with his quick, emphatic *Chew-che-rick* or *Che-rick-a-rew*, flitted and ducked and hid among the low bushes by the roadside. A girl told me she had heard the nightingale yesterday on her way to Sunday-school, and pointed out the spot. It was in some bushes near a house. I hovered about this place till I was afraid the woman, who saw me from the window, would think I had some designs upon her premises. But I managed to look very indifferent or abstracted when I passed. I am quite sure I heard the chiding, guttural note of the bird I was after. Doubtless her brood had come out that very day. Another girl had heard a nightingale on her way to school that morning, and directed me to the road; still another pointed out to me the whitethroat and said that was my bird. This last was a rude shock to my faith in the ornithology of schoolgirls. Finally, I found a laborer breaking stone by the roadside,—a serious, honest-faced man, who said he had heard my bird that morning on his way to work; he heard her every morning, and nearly every night, too. He heard her last night after the shower (just at the hour when my barber and I were trying to awaken her near Hazlemere), and she sang as finely as ever she did. This was a great lift. I felt that I could trust this man. He said that after his day's work was done, that is, at five o'clock, if I chose to accompany him on his way home, he would show me where he had heard the bird. This I gladly agreed to; and, remembering that I had had no dinner, I sought out the inn in the village and asked for something to eat. The unwonted request so startled the landlord that he came out from behind his inclosed bar and confronted me with good-humored curiosity. These back-country English inns, as I several times found to my discomfiture, are only drinking places for the accommodation of local customers, mainly of the laboring class. Instead of standing conspicuously on some street corner, as with us, they usually stand on some byway, or some little paved court away from the main thoroughfare. I could have plenty of beer, said the landlord, but he had not a mouthful of meat in the house. I urged my needs, and finally got some rye-bread and cheese. With this and a glass of home-brewed beer I was fairly well fortified. At the appointed time I met the cottager and went with him on his way home. We walked two miles or more along a charming road, full of wooded nooks and arbor-like vistas. Why do English trees always look so sturdy, and exhibit such massive repose, so unlike, in this latter respect, to the nervous and agitated expression of most of our own foliage? Probably because they have been a long time out of the woods, and have had plenty of room in which to develop individual traits and peculiarities; then, in a deep fertile soil, and a climate that does not hurry or overtax, they grow slow and last long, and

come to have the picturesqueness of age without its infirmities.
The oak, the elm, the beech, all have more striking profiles
than in our country.

Presently my companion pointed out to me a small wood
below the road that had a wide fringe of bushes and saplings
connecting it with a meadow, amid which stood the tree-
embowered house of a city man, where he had heard the nightingale in the morning; and then, farther along, showed me,
near his own cottage, where he had heard one the evening
before. It was now only six o'clock, and I had two or three
hours to wait before I could reasonably expect to hear her. "It
gets to be into the hevening," said my new friend, "when she
sings the most, you know." I whiled away the time as best I
could. If I had been an artist, I should have brought away a
sketch of a picturesque old cottage near by, that bore the date
of 1688 on its wall. I was obliged to keep moving most of the
time to keep warm. Yet the "no-see-'ems," or midges, annoyed
me, in a temperature which at home would have chilled them
buzzless and biteless. Finally, I leaped the smooth masonry
of the stone wall and ambushed myself amid the tall ferns
under a pine-tree, where the nightingale had been heard in
the morning. If the keeper had seen me, he would probably
have taken me for a poacher. I sat shivering there till nine
o'clock, listening to the cooing of the wood-pigeons, watching
the motions of a jay that, I suspect, had a nest near by, and
taking note of various other birds. The song-thrush and the
robins soon made such a musical uproar along the borders of
a grove, across an adjoining field, as quite put me out. It might
veil and obscure the one voice I wanted to hear. The robin
continued to sing quite into the darkness. This bird is related
to the nightingale, and looks and acts like it at a little distance;

and some of its notes are remarkably piercing and musical. When my patience was about exhausted, I was startled by a quick, brilliant call or whistle, a few rods from me, that at once recalled my barber with his blade of grass, and I knew my long-sought bird was inflating her throat. How it woke me up! It had the quality that startles; it pierced the gathering gloom like a rocket. Then it ceased. Suspecting I was too near the singer, I moved away cautiously, and stood in a lane beside the wood, where a loping hare regarded me a few paces away. Then my singer struck up again, but I could see did not let herself out; just tuning her instrument, I thought, and getting ready to transfix the silence and the darkness. A little later, a man and boy came up the lane. I asked them if that was the nightingale singing; they listened, and assured me it was none other. "Now she's on, sir; now she's on. Ah! but she don't stick. In May, sir, they makes the woods all heccho about here. Now she's on again; that's her, sir; now she's off; she won't stick." And stick she would not. I could hear a hoarse wheezing and clucking sound beneath her notes, when I listened intently. The man and boy moved away. I stood mutely invoking all the gentle divinities to spur the bird on. Just then a bird like our hermit thrush came quickly over the hedge a few yards below me, swept close past my face, and back into the thicket. I had been caught listening; the offended bird had found me taking notes of her dry and worn-out pipe there behind the hedge, and the concert abruptly ended; not another note; not a whisper. I waited a long time and then moved off; then came back, implored the outraged bird to resume; then rushed off, and slammed the door, or rather the gate, indignantly behind me. I paused by other shrines, but not a sound. The cottager had told me of a little village three miles beyond,

where there were three inns, and where I could probably get
lodgings for the night. I walked rapidly in that direction; committed myself to a footpath; lost the trail, and brought up at a
little cottage in a wide expanse of field or common, and by the
good woman, with a babe in her arms, was set right again. I
soon struck the highway by the bridge, as I had been told,
and a few paces brought me to the first inn. It was ten o'clock,
and the lights were just about to be put out, as the law or
custom is in country inns. The landlady said she could not
give me a bed; she had only one spare room, and that was not
in order, and she should not set about putting it in shape at
that hour; and she was short and sharp about it, too. I hastened
on to the next one. The landlady said she had no sheets, and
the bed was damp and unfit to sleep in. I protested that I
thought an inn was an inn, and for the accommodation of
travelers. But she referred me to the next house. Here were
more people, and more the look and air of a public house. But
the wife (the man does not show himself on such occasions)
said her daughter had just got married and come home, and
she had much company and could not keep me. In vain I urged
my extremity; there was no room. Could I have something to
eat, then? This seemed doubtful, and led to consultations in
the kitchen; but, finally, some bread and cold meat were produced. The nearest hotel was Godalming, seven miles distant,
and I knew all the inns would be shut up before I could get
there. So I munched my bread and meat, consoling myself
with the thought that perhaps this was just the ill wind that
would blow me the good I was in quest of. I saw no alternative
but to spend a night under the trees with the nightingales; and
I might surprise them at their revels in the small hours of the
morning. Just as I was ready to congratulate myself on the

richness of my experience, the landlady came in and said there
was a young man there going with a "trap" to Godalming, and
he had offered to take me in. I feared I should pass for an
escaped lunatic if I declined the offer; so I reluctantly assented,
and we were presently whirling through the darkness, along a
smooth, winding road, toward town. The young man was a
drummer; was from Lincolnshire, and said I spoke like a Lincolnshire man. I could believe it, for I told him he talked more
like an American than any native I had met. The hotels in the
larger towns close at eleven, and I was set down in front of
one just as the clock was striking that hour. I asked to be
conducted to a room at once. As I was about getting in bed
there was a rap at the door, and a waiter presented me my bill
on a tray. "Gentlemen as have no luggage, etc." he explained;
and pretend to be looking for nightingales, too! Three-and-
sixpence; two shillings for the bed and one-and-six for service.
I was out at five in the morning, before any one inside was
astir. After much trying of bars and doors, I made my exit into
a paved court, from which a covered way led into the street.
A man opened a window and directed me how to undo the
great door, and forth I started, still hoping to catch my bird
at her matins. I took the route of the day before. On the edge
of the beautiful plowed field, looking down through the trees
and bushes into the gleam of the river twenty rods below, I
was arrested by the note I longed to hear. It came up from
near the water, and made my ears tingle. I folded up my rubber
coat and sat down upon it, saying, Now we will take our fill.
But—the bird ceased, and, tarry though I did for an hour, not
another note reached me. The prize seemed destined to elude
me each time just as I thought it mine. Still, I treasured what
little I had heard.

It was enough to convince me of the superior quality of the song, and make me more desirous than ever to hear the complete strain. I continued my rambles, and in the early morning once more hung about the Shackerford copses and loitered along the highways. Two schoolboys pointed out a tree to me in which they had heard the nightingale, on their way for milk, two hours before. But I could only repeat Emerson's lines:—

> "Right good-will my sinews strung,
> But no speed of mine avails
> To hunt up their shining trails."

At nine o'clock I gave over the pursuit and returned to Easing in quest of breakfast. Bringing up in front of the large and comfortable-looking inn, I found the mistress of the house with her daughter engaged in washing windows. Perched upon their step-ladders, they treated my request for breakfast very coldly; in fact, finally refused to listen to it at all. The fires were out, and I could not be served. So I must continue my walk back to Godalming; and, in doing so, I found that one may walk three miles on indignation quite as easily as upon bread.

In the afternoon I returned to my lodgings at Shotter Mill, and made ready for a walk to Selborne, twelve miles distant, part of the way to be accomplished that night in the gloaming, and the rest early on the following morning, to give the nightingales a chance to make any reparation they might feel inclined to for the neglect with which they had treated me. There was a footpath over the hill and through Leechmere bottom to Liphook, and to this, with the sun half an hour high, I committed myself. The feature in this hill scenery of Surrey and Sussex that is new to American eyes is given by the furze and heather, broad black or dark-brown patches of which sweep over the high rolling surfaces, like sable mantles. Tennyson's house stands amid this dusky scenery, a few miles east of Hazlemere. The path led through a large common, partly covered with grass and partly grown up to furze,—another un-American feature. Doubly precious is land in England, and yet so much of it given to parks and pleasure-grounds, and so much of it left unreclaimed in commons! These commons are frequently met with; about Selborne they are miles in extent, and embrace the Hanger and other woods. No one can inclose them, or appropriate them to his own use. The landed proprietor of whose estates they form a part cannot; they belong to the people, to the lease-holders. The villagers and others who own houses on leased land pasture their cows upon them, gather the furze, and cut the wood. In some places the commons belong to the crown and are crown lands. These large uninclosed spaces often give a free-and-easy air to the landscape that is very welcome. Near the top of the hill I met a little old man nearly hidden beneath a burden of furze. He was backing it home for fuel and other uses. He paused obsequious, and listened to my inquiries. A dwarfish sort of man, whose ugliness was redolent of the humblest chimney corner. Bent beneath his bulky burden, and grinning upon me, he was a visible embodiment of the poverty, ignorance, and, I may say, the domesticity of the lowliest peasant home. I felt as if I had encountered a walking superstition, fostered beside a hearth lighted by furze fagots and by branches dropped by the nesting rooks and ravens,—a figure half repulsive and half alluring. On the border of Leechmere bottom I sat down above a straggling copse, aflame as usual with the foxglove, and gave eye and ear to the scene. While sitting here, I saw and heard for the first time the black-capped warbler. I recognized the note at once by its brightness and strength, and a faint suggestion in it of the nightingale's. But it was disappointing: I had expected a nearer approach to its great rival. The bird was very shy, but did finally show herself fairly several times, as she did also near Selborne, where I heard the song oft repeated and prolonged. It is a ringing, animated strain, but as a whole seemed to me crude, not smoothly and finely modulated. I could name several of our own birds that surpass it in pure music. Like its congeners, the garden warbler and the white-throat, it sings with great emphasis and strength, but its song is silvern, not golden. "Little birds with big voices," one says to himself after having heard most of the British songsters. My path led me an adventurous course through the copses and bottoms and open commons, in the long twilight. At one point I came upon three young men standing together and watching a dog that was working a near field,—one of them probably the squire's son, and the other two habited like laborers. In a little thicket near by there was a brilliant chorus of bird voices, the robin, the songthrush, and the blackbird, all vying with each other. To my inquiry, put to test the reliability of the young countrymen's ears, they replied that one of the birds I heard was the nightingale, and, after a moment's attention, singled out the robin as the bird in question. This incident so impressed me that I paid little attention to the report of the next man I met, who said he had heard a nightingale just around a bend in the road, a few minutes' walk in advance of me. At ten o'clock I reached Liphook. I expected and half hoped the inn would turn its back upon me again, in which case I proposed to make for Wolmer Forest, a few miles distant, but it did not. Before going to bed, I took a short and hasty walk down a promising-looking lane, and again met a couple who had heard nightingales. "It was a nightingale, was it not, Charley?"

If all the people of whom I inquired for nightingales in England could have been together and compared notes, they probably would not have been long in deciding that there was at least one crazy American abroad.

I proposed to be up and off at five o'clock in the morning, which seemed greatly to puzzle mine host. At first he thought it could not be done, but finally saw his way out of the dilemma, and said he would get up and undo the door for me himself. The morning was cloudy and misty, though the previous night had been of the fairest. There is one thing they do not have in England that we can boast of at home, and that is a good masculine type of weather: it is not even feminine; it is childish and puerile, though I am told that occasionally there is a full-grown storm. But I saw nothing but petulant little showers and prolonged juvenile sulks. The clouds have no reserve, no dignity; if there is a drop of water in them (and there generally are several drops), out it comes. The prettiest little showers march across the country in summer, scarcely bigger than a street watering-cart; sometimes by getting over the fence one can avoid them, but they keep the haymakers in a perpetual flurry. There is no cloud scenery, as with us, no mass and solidity, no height nor depth. The clouds seem low, vague, and vapory,—immature, indefinite, inconsequential, like youth.

The walk to Selborne was through mist and light rain. Few bird voices, save the cries of the lapwing and the curlew, were heard. Shortly after leaving Liphook the road takes a straight cut for three or four miles through a level, black, barren, peaty stretch of country, with Wolmer Forest a short distance on the right. Under the low-hanging clouds the scene was a dismal one,—a black earth beneath and a gloomy sky above. For miles the only sign of life was a baker's cart rattling along the smooth, white road. At the end of this solitude I came to cultivated fields, and a little hamlet and an inn. At this inn (for a wonder!) I got some breakfast. The family had not yet had theirs, and I sat with them at the table, and had substantial fare. From this point I followed a footpath a couple of miles through fields and parks. The highways for the most part seemed so narrow and exclusive, or inclusive, such penalties seemed to attach to a view over the high walls and hedges that shut me in, that a footpath was always a welcome escape to me. I opened the wicket or mounted the stile without much concern as to whether it would further me on my way or not. It was like turning the flank of an enemy. These well-kept fields and lawns, these cozy nooks, these stately and exclusive houses that had taken such pains to shut out the public gaze,—from the footpath one had them at an advantage, and could pluck out their mystery. On striking the highway again, I met the postmistress, stepping briskly along with the morning mail. Her husband had died, and she had taken his place as mail-carrier. England is so densely populated, the country is so like a great city suburb, that your mail is brought to your door everywhere, the same as in town. I walked a distance with a boy driving a little old white horse with a cart-load of brick. He lived at Hedleigh, six miles distant; he had left there at five o'clock in the morning, and had heard a nightingale. He was sure; as I pressed him, he described the place minutely. "She was in the large fir-tree by Tom Anthony's gate, at the south end of the village." Then, I said, doubtless I shall find one in some of Gilbert White's haunts; but I did not. I spent two rainy days at Selborne; I passed many chilly and cheerless hours loitering along those wet lanes and dells and dripping hangers, wooing both my bird and the spirit of the gentle parson, but apparently without getting very near to either. When I think of the place now, I see its hurrying and anxious haymakers in the field of mown grass, and hear the cry of a child that sat in the hay back of the old church, and cried by the hour while its mother was busy with her rake not far off. The rain had ceased, the hay had dried off a little, and scores of men, women, and children, but mostly women, had flocked to the fields to rake it up. The hay is got together inch by inch, and every inch is fought for. They first rake it up into narrow swaths, each person taking a strip about a yard wide. If they hold the ground thus gained, when the hay dries an hour or two longer, they take another hitch, and thus on till they get it into the cock or "carry" it from the windrow. It is usually nearly worn out with handling before they get it into the rick.

From Selborne I went to Alton, along a road that was one prolonged rifle-pit, but smooth and hard as a rock; thence by train back to London. To leave no ground for self-accusation in future, on the score of not having made a thorough effort to hear my songster, I the next day made a trip north toward Cambridge, leaving the train at Hitchin, a large picturesque old town, and thought myself in just the right place at last. I found a road between the station and the town proper called Nightingale Lane, famous for its songsters. A man who kept a thrifty-looking inn on the corner (where, by the way, I was again refused both bed and board) said they sang night and morning in the trees opposite. He had heard them the night before, but had not noticed them that morning. He often sat at night with his friends, with open windows, listening to the strain. He said he had tried several times to hold his breath as long as the bird did in uttering certain notes, but could not do it. This, I knew, was an exaggeration; but I waited eagerly for nightfall, and, when it came, paced the street like a patrolman, and paced other streets, and lingered about other likely localities, but caught nothing but neuralgic pains in my shoulder. I had no better success in the morning, and here gave over the pursuit, saying to myself, It matters little, after all; I have seen the country and had some object for a walk, and that is sufficient.

Altogether I heard the bird less than five minutes, and only a few bars of its song, but enough to satisfy me of the surprising quality of the strain.

It had the master tone as clearly as Tennyson or any great prima donna or famous orator has it. Indeed, it was just the same. Here is the complete artist, of whom all these other birds are but hints and studies. Bright, startling, assured, of great compass and power, it easily dominates all other notes; the harsher *chur-r-r-rg* notes serve as foil to her surpassing brilliancy. Wordsworth, among the poets, has hit off the song nearest:—

> "Those notes of thine,—they pierce and pierce;
> Tumultuous harmony and fierce!"

I could easily understand that this bird might keep people awake at night by singing near their houses, as I was assured it frequently does; there is something in the strain so startling and awakening. Its start is a vivid flash of sound. On the whole, a high-bred, courtly, chivalrous song; a song for ladies to hear leaning from embowered windows on moonlight nights; a song for royal parks and groves,—and easeful but impassioned life.

We have no bird-voice so piercing and loud, with such flexibility and compass, such full-throated harmony and long-drawn cadences; though we have songs of more melody, tenderness, and plaintiveness. None but the nightingale could have inspired Keats's ode,—that longing for self-forgetfulness and for the oblivion of the world, to escape the fret and fever of life.

"And with thee fade away into the forest dim."

IN FIELD AND WOOD:
INTENSIVE OBSERVATION

The casual glances or the admiring glances that we cast upon nature do not go very far in making us acquainted with her real ways. Only long and close scrutiny can reveal these to us. The look of appreciation is not enough; the eye must become critical and analytical if we would know the exact truth.

Close scrutiny of an object in nature will nearly always yield some significant fact that our admiring gaze did not take in. I learned a new fact about the teazel the other day by scrutinizing it more closely than I had ever before done; I discovered that the wave of bloom begins in the middle of the head and spreads both ways, up and down, whereas in all other plants known to me with flowering heads or spikes, except the goldenrod and the steeplebush, the wave of bloom begins at the bottom and creeps upward like a flame. In the goldenrod it drops down from branch to branch. In vervain, in blue-weed, in Venus' looking-glass, in the mullein, in the evening-primrose, and others, the bloom creeps slowly upward from the bottom.

But with the teazel the flame of bloom is first kindled in the middle; to-day you see the head with this purple zone or girdle about it, and in a day or two you see two purple girdles with an open space between them, and these move, the one up and the other down, till the head stands with a purple base and a purple crown with a broad space of neutral green between them.

This is a sample of the small but significant facts in nature that interest me—exceptional facts that show how nature at times breaks away from a fixed habit, a beaten path, so to speak, and tries a new course. She does this in animal life too.

Huxley mentions a curious exception to the general plan of the circulation of the blood. In all animals that have a circulation the blood takes one definite and invariable direction except in the case of one class of marine animals, called ascidians; in them the heart, after beating a certain number of times, stops and begins to beat the opposite way, so as to reverse the current; then in a moment or two it changes again and drives the blood in the other direction.

All things are possible with nature, and these unexpected possibilities or departures from the general plan are very interesting. It is interesting to know that any creature can come into being without a father, but with only a grandfather, yet such is the case. The drone in the hive has no father; the eggs of the unfertilized queen produce drones—that is, in producing males, the male is dispensed with. It is to produce the neuters or the workers that the service of the male is required. The queen bee is developed from one of these neuter eggs, hence her male offspring have only a grandfather.

The chipmunk is an old friend of my boyhood and my later

years also, but by scrutinizing his ways a little more closely than usual the past summer I learned things about this pretty little rodent that I did not before know. I discovered, for instance, that he digs his new hole for his winter quarters in midsummer.

In my strolls afield or along the road in July I frequently saw a fresh pile of earth upon the grass near a stone fence, or in the orchard, or on the edge of the woods—usually a peck or two of bright, new earth carefully put down in a pile upon the ground without any clue visible as to where it probably came from. But a search in the grass or leaves usually disclosed its source—a little round hole neatly cut through the turf and leading straight downward. I came upon ten such mounds of earth upon a single farm, and found the hole from which each came, from one to six feet away. In one case, in a meadow recently mowed, I had to explore the stubble with my finger over several square yards of surface before I found the squirrel's hole, so undisturbed was the grass around it; not a grain of soil had the little delver dropped near it, and not the slightest vestige of a path had he made from the tunnel to the dump.

And this feature was noticeable in every case; the hole had been dug several yards under ground and several pecks of fresh earth removed to a distance of some feet without the least speck of soil or the least trace of the workman's footsteps showing near the entrance; such clean, deft workmanship was remarkable. All this half-bushel or more of earth the squirrel must have carried out in his cheek pockets, and he must have made hundreds of trips to and fro from his dump to his hole, and yet if he had flown like a bird the turf could not have been freer from the marks of his going and coming; and he had cut down through the turf as one might have done with an auger, without bruising or disturbing in any way the grass about the edges. It was a clean, neat job in every case, so much so that it was hard to believe that the delver did not come up from below and have a back door from whence he carried his soil some yards away.

Indeed, I have heard this theory stated. "Look under the pile of earth," said a friend who was with me and who had observed the work of the pocket gopher in the West, "and you will find the back door there." But it was not so. I carefully removed four piles of earth and dug away the turf beneath them, and no hole was to be found.

One day we found a pile of earth in a meadow, and near it a hole less than two inches deep, showing where the chipmunk had begun to dig and had struck a stone; then he went a foot or more up the hill and began again; here he soon struck stones as before, then he went still farther up the hill, and this time was successful in penetrating the soil. This was conclusive proof that these round holes are cut from above and not from below, as we often see in the case of the woodchuck-hole. The squirrel apparently gnaws through the turf, instead of digging through, and carries away the loosened material in his mouth, never dropping or scattering a grain of it. No home was ever built with less litter, no cleaner dooryard from first to last can be found.

The absence of anything like a trail or beaten way from the mound of earth to the hole, or anything suggesting passing feet, I understood better when, later in the season, day after day I saw a chipmunk carrying supplies into his den, which was in the turf by the roadside about ten feet from a stone wall. He covered the distance by a series of short jumps, apparently striking each time upon his toes between the spears of grass, and leaving no marks whatever by which his course could be traced. This was also his manner of leaving the hole, and doubtless it was his manner in carrying away the soil from his tunnel to the dumping-pile. He left no sign upon the grass, he disturbed not one spear about the entrance.

There was a mystery about this den by the roadside of which I have just spoken—the pile of earth could not be found; unless the roadmaker had removed it, it must have been hidden in or beneath the stone wall.

And there was a mystery about some of the other holes that was absolutely baffling to me. In at least four mounds of fresh earth I found freshly dug stones that I could not by any manipulation get back into the hole out of which they had evidently come. They were all covered with fresh earth, and were in the pile of soil with many other smaller stones. In one case a stone two inches long, one and one half inches broad, and one half inch thick was found. In two other cases stones of about the same length and breadth but not so thick were found, and in neither case could the stone be forced into the hole. In still another case the entrance to the den was completely framed by the smaller roots of a beech-tree, and in the little mound of earth near it were two stones that could only be gotten back into the hole by springing one of these roots, which required considerable force to do. In two at least of these four cases it was a physical impossibility for the stones to have come out of the hole from whence the mound of earth and the lesser stones evidently came, yet how happened they in the pile of earth freshly earth-stained? The squirrel could not have carried them in his cheek pouches, they were so large; how, then, did he carry them?

The matter stood thus with me for some weeks; I was up

against a little problem in natural history that I could not solve. Late in November I visited the scene of the squirrel-holes again, and at last got the key to the mystery: the cunning little delver cuts a groove in one side of the hole just large enough to let the stone through, then packs it full of soil again. When I made my November visit it had been snowing and raining and freezing and thawing, and the top of the ground was getting soft. A red squirrel had visited the hole in the orchard where two of the largest stones were found in the pile of earth, and had apparently tried to force his way into the chipmunk's den. In doing so he had loosened the earth in the groove, softened by the rains, and it had dropped out. The groove was large enough for me to lay my finger in and just adequate to admit the stones into the hole. This, then, was the way the little engineer solved the problem, and I experienced a sense of relief that I had solved mine.

I visited the second hole where the large stone was in the pile of earth, and found that the same thing had happened there. A red squirrel, bent on plunder, had been trying to break in, and had removed the soil in the groove.*

To settle the point as to whether or not the chipmunk has a back door, which in no case had I been able to find, we dug out the one by the roadside, whose mound of earth we could not discover. We followed his tortuous course through the soil three or four feet from the entrance and nearly three feet beneath the surface, where we found him in his chamber, warm in his nest of leaves, but not asleep. He had no back door.

---

* I feel bound to report that the next season I found a pile of earth which a chipmunk had removed from his den, containing a stone too large to go into the hole, yet the most careful examination failed to reveal that there had ever been any groove cut in it, or that it had ever been in any way enlarged.

He came out (it was a male) as a hand was thrust into his chamber, and the same fearless, strong hand seized him, but did not hurt him. His chamber was spacious enough to hold about four quarts of winter stores and leave him considerable room to stir about in. His supplies consisted of the seeds of the wild buckwheat (*Polygonum dumetorum*) and choke-cherry pits, and formed a very unpromising looking mess. His buckwheat did not seem to have been properly cured, for much of it was mouldy, but it had been carefully cleaned, every kernel of it. There were nearly four quarts of seeds altogether, and over one half of it was wild buckwheat. I was curious to know approximately the number of these seeds he had gathered and shucked. I first found the number it took to fill a lady's thimble, and then the number of thimbles full it took to fill a cup, and so reached the number in the two quarts, and found that it amounted to the surprising figure of 250,000.

Think of the amount of patient labor required to clean 250,000 of the small seeds of the wild buckwheat! The grains are hardly one third the size of those of the cultivated kind and are jet black when the husk is removed. Probably every seed was husked with those deft little hands and teeth as it was gathered, before it went into his cheek pockets, but what a task it must have been!

Poor little hermit, it seemed pathetic to find him facing the coming winter there with such inferior stuff in his granary. Not a nut, not a kernel of corn or wheat. Why he had not availed himself of the oats that grew just over the fence I should like to know. Of course, the wild buckwheat must have been more to his liking. How many hazardous trips along fences and into the bushes his stores represented! The wild creatures all live in as savage a country as did our earliest ancestors, and the enemy of each is lying in wait for it at nearly every turn.

Digging the little fellow out, of course, brought ruin upon his house, and I think the Muse of Natural History contemplated the scene with many compunctions of conscience,—if she has any conscience, which I am inclined to doubt. But our human hearts prompted us to do all we could to give the provident little creature a fresh start; we put his supplies carefully down beside the stone wall into which he had disappeared on being liberated, and the next day he had carried a large part of them away. He evidently began at once to "hustle," and I trust he found or made a new retreat from the winter before it was too late.

I doubt if the chipmunk ever really hibernates; the hibernating animals do not lay up winter stores, but he no doubt indulges in many very long before-dinner and after-dinner naps. It is blackest night there in his den three feet under the ground, and this lasts about four months, or until the premonitions of coming spring reach him in March and call him forth.

I am curious to know if the female chipmunk also digs a den for herself, or takes up with one occupied by the male the previous winter.

One ought to be safe in generalizing upon the habits of chipmunks in digging their holes, after observing ten of them, yet one must go slow even then. Nine of the holes I observed had a pile of earth near them; the tenth hole had no dump that I could find. Then I found four holes with the soil hauled out and piled up about the entrance precisely after the manner of woodchucks. This was a striking exception to the general habit of the chipmunk in this matter. "Is this the way the female digs her hole," I asked myself, "or is it the work of young chipmunks?"

I have in two cases found holes in the ground on the borders of swamps, occupied by weasels, but the holes were in all outward respects like those made by chipmunks, with no soil near the entrance. The woodchuck makes no attempt to conceal his hole by carrying away the soil; neither does the prairie-dog, nor the pocket gopher. The pile of telltale earth in each case may be seen from afar, but our little squirrel seems to have notions of neatness and concealment that he rarely departs from. The more I study his ways, the more I see what a clever and foxy little rodent he is.

IN "THE CIRCUIT OF
THE SUMMER HILLS"

I

To sit on one's rustic porch, or at the door of one's tent, and see the bees working on the catnip or motherwort or clover, to see the cattle grazing leisurely in the fields or ruminating under the spreading trees, or the woodchucks creeping about the meadows and pastures, or the squirrels spinning along the fences, or the hawks describing great spirals against the sky; to hear no sound but the voice of birds, the caw of crows, the whistle of marmots, the chirp of crickets; to smell no odors but the odors of grassy fields, or blooming meadows, or falling rain; amid it all, to lift one's eyes to the flowing and restful mountain lines—this is to get a taste of the peace and comfort of the summer hills.

This boon is mine when I go to my little gray farmhouse on a broad hill-slope on the home farm in the Catskills. Especially is it mine when, to get still nearer nature and beyond the orbit of household sounds and interruptions, I retreat to the big hay-barn, and on an improvised table in front of the big open barn doors, looking out into the sunlit fields where I hoed corn or made hay as a boy, I write this and other papers.

The peace of the hills is about me and upon me, and the leisure of the summer clouds, whose shadows I see slowly drifting across the face of the landscape, is mine. The dissonance and the turbulence and the stenches of cities—how far off they seem! the noise and the dust and the acrimony of politics—how completely the hum of the honey-bees and the twitter of swallows blot them all out!

In the circuit of the hills, the days take form and character as they do not in town, or in a country of low horizons. George Eliot says in one of her letters: "In the country the days have broad open spaces, and the very stillness seems to give a delightful roominess to the hours." This is especially true in a hilly and mountainous country, where the eye has a great depth of perspective opened to it. Take those extra brilliant days that we so often have in the autumn—what a vivid sense one gets of their splendor amid the hills! The deep, cradle-like valleys, and the long flowing mountain lines, make a fit receptacle for the day's beauty; they hold and accumulate it, as it were. I think of Emerson's line:—

"Oh, tenderly the haughty day fills his blue urn with fire."

The valleys are vast blue urns that hold a generous portion of the lucid hours!

To feel to the full the peace of the hills, one must choose his hills, and see to it that they are gentle and restful in character. Abruptness, jagged lines, sharp angles, frowning precipices, while they may add an element of picturesqueness, interfere with the feeling of ease and restfulness that the peace of the hills implies. The eye is disturbed by a confusion of broken and abrupt lines as is the ear by a volume of discordant sounds. Long, undulating mountain lines, broad, cradle-like valleys, easy basking hill-slopes, as well as the absence of loud and discordant sounds, are a factor in the restfulness of any landscape.

My landscape is very old geologically, as old as the order of vertebrate animals, but young historically, having been settled only about one hundred and fifty years. The original forests still cover the tops of the mountains with a dark-green mantle, which comes well down upon their sides, where it is cut and torn and notched into by the upper fields of the valley farms.

I call my place Woodchuck Lodge, as I tell my friends, because we are beleagured by these rodents. There is a cordon of woodchuck-holes all around us. In the orchard, in the meadows, in the pastures, these whistling marmots have their dens. Here one might easily have woodchuck venison for dinner every day, yea, and for supper and breakfast, too, if one could acquire a taste for it. I tried to dine on a woodchuck once when I was a boy, but never have felt inclined to repeat the experiment. If one were born in the woods and lived in the woods, maybe he could relish a woodchuck. Talk about being autochthonous, and savoring of the soil—try a woodchuck! The feeding habits of this animal are as cleanly as those of a sheep or a cow; clover, plantain, peas, beans, cucumbers, cabbages, apples —all sweet and succulent things—go to the making of his flabby body; yet he spends so much of his time in pickle in the ground that his flesh is rank with the earth flavor. He is not lean like a rabbit or a squirrel, nor so firm of muscle as a 'coon or a 'possum; he is little more than a skin filled with viscera. He is busy all summer storing up fat in his loose pouch of a body for fuel during his long winter sleep. This sleep appears to begin in late September, or after the first white frost. This year I saw my last specimen on the 28th of the month as he was running in great haste to his hole. Evidently he does not like the pinch of the cold. He is a fair-weather animal and is the epicure of the meadows and pastures. While the apples are still mellow on the ground, while the red thorn is still dropping its fruit, and the aftermath is still fresh in the meadows, my woodchucks turn their backs upon the world and retreat to their underground chambers for their six months' slumber. I know of no other hibernating animal that retires from the light of day so early in the season. His active life stretches from the vernal equinox to the autumnal equinox, and that is about all. Half the year he is under ground, and at least half of each summer day. No wonder his flesh is rank with the earth flavor. He appears to live only to accumulate his winter store of fat. Apparently he comes out of his den in summer only to feed, and maybe occasionally to bask in the sunshine. He is never sportive or discursive like the birds and squirrels. Life is a very serious business with him, and he has reduced it to the lowest terms—eat, breed, and sleep. If woodchucks ever engage in any sort of play, like other wild creatures, I never have seen them, though I once had a tame young 'chuck that would play with the kitten.

The woodchuck probably sleeps more than half the time in summer; he economizes his precious fat. Only once have I seen his tracks on the snow. This was in late December; and, following them up, I found the woodchuck wandering about the meadow like one half demented. Something had evidently gone wrong with him. Apparently he had not succeeded in storing up his usual amount of fat. He showed little fight, and we picked him up by the tail, put him into the sleigh, and brought him home. A place under the barn floor was given to him, but he did not long survive. All the glory of the fall, the heyday of the 'coon and the squirrels, the woodchuck misses. No golden October, no Indian summer for him; he has had his day.

Though the woodchuck's muscles are flabby, his heart is stout. The farm-dog can kill him, but he cannot make him show fear or dismay; he is game to the last. Twice I have seen him from my porch at Woodchuck Lodge put on so bold a front and become so aggressive, when surprised in the middle of a field by a big shepherd-dog, that the dog did not dare attack him, but circled about, seeking some unfair advantage, only to be met at every point with those threatening, grating teeth. The woodchuck was far from his hole, and he kept charging the dog and driving him nearer and nearer the stone wall, where his own safety lay. An observer inoculated with the idea of animal reason would have said that the tactics of the 'chuck were premeditated; but I am sure he was too much engrossed with the task of defending himself from the jaws of that dog to do any logical thinking or planning. It was only the fortune of battle that finally brought the hunter and the hunted near the hole of safety, when, seeing his chance, the woodchuck made a sudden, successful dash, too hurried, I fancy, even to whistle his usual note of defiance. In the other case, the dog was of a still more timid nature, and when the surprised woodchuck showed fight, he concluded that he had no business at all with that particular 'chuck, which actually chased him from the meadow. I can still see the woodchuck's bristling, expanded tail as he drove fiercely after the fleeing dog, which, with a tail anything but threatening, escaped over the wall into the road.

I find that one may be the principal actor in a little comedy, and not see the humor of it at all at the time. I know the humor of a race I had with a 'chuck last summer in my orchard was quite lost upon me till it was over, when the 'chuck was in his hole, and I was back upon my porch recovering my wind. The 'chuck was a hundred yards or more from his den when I leaped over the fence from the road and surprised him. I pressed him so closely that he took refuge in an apple-tree. Instantly seeing his mistake, as the missile I hurled struck the tree, he sprang down and rushed for his hole, a hundred and fifty feet away. But I got there first. The 'chuck paused twenty feet to one side and regarded me intently, defiantly. We stood and glared at each other a few moments, while I recovered my breath. I wanted the scalp of that "varmint." I knew that he would make himself believe that I had planted my garden for his special benefit, and I wanted to anticipate that conclusion. I was weaponless. Twenty or more feet from me, on the opposite side from the 'chuck, I saw a stone that would answer my purpose. I calculated the chances; so did the woodchuck; I sprang for the stone and the 'chuck sprang for his hole, and was in it as my hand touched the stone. He had won! As I sat on my porch, the recklessness and absurdity of a man more than threescore and ten running down a woodchuck came over me; and I have not yielded to such a temptation since.

II

Where cattle and woodchucks thrive, there thrive I. The pastoral is in my veins. Clover and timothy, daisies and buttercups indirectly colored my youthful life; and if the dairy cow did not rock my cradle, her products sustained the hand that did rock it. Hence I love this land of wide, open, grassy fields, of smooth, broad-backed hills, and of long, flowing mountain lines. The cow fits well into these scenes. It seems as if her broad, smooth muzzle and her sweeping tongue might have shaped the landscape; it is certainly her cropping that has brought about the hourglass form of so many of the red thorn trees, which give a unique feature to the fields. Her fragrant breath is upon the air, her hoof-prints are upon the highway; she may not yet have attained to wisdom, yet surely all her ways are ways of pleasantness and all her paths are paths of peace. Hence, when her ways and her paths coincide with mine, I thrive best. From Woodchuck Lodge I look out upon broad pastures, lands where dairy herds have grazed for a hundred years, never the same herd for many summers, but all of the same habits and dispositions. They all scour the pastures in the same way, scattering, searching out every nook and corner, leaving no yard of ground unvisited, apparently hunting each day for the sweet morsel they missed the day before, disposing themselves in picturesque groups upon the hills; never massed, except under the shade-trees on hot days; slow-moving, making their paths here and there, lingering under the red thorn trees, where the fruit begins to drop in September; tossing their heads above the orchard wall, where the fragrance of ripening apples is on the air; in the autumn lying upon the cold, damp ground and ruminating contentedly, with no fear of our ills and pains before them; wading in the swamps, converging slowly toward the pasture-bars as milking-time draws nigh, with always some tardy, indifferent ones that the farm-dog has to hurry up; many-colored,—white, black, red, brown,—at times showing rare gentleness and affection toward one another, such as licking one another's heads or bodies, then spitefully butting or goring one another; occasionally one of them lifting up her head and sending her mellow voice over the hills like a horn, as if to give voice to a vague unrest, or invoking some far-off divinity to release the imprisoned Io—what a series of shifting rural pictures I thus have spread out before me! Such an atmosphere of peace and leisure over it all! The unhurrying and ruminating cattle make the days long; they make the fields friendly, the hills eloquent, the shade-trees idyllic. I wake up to hear the farmer summoning them from the field in the dewy summer dawns, and I listen for his call to them on the tranquil afternoons. One season an especially musical voice did the evening calling—a trained voice from beyond the hills. What a pleasure it was as we swung in our hammocks under the apple-trees to hear the free, sonorous summons, and to see the response of the herd in many-colored lines converging down the slope to the barway!

When the meadows have gotten a new carpet of tender grass in September, and the cows are free to range in them, a new series of moving pictures greets the eye. The grazing forms have a finer setting now, and contentment and satisfaction are in every movement. How they sweep off the tender herbage, into what artistic groups they naturally fall, what pictures of peace and plenty they present! When they lie down to ruminate, Emerson's sentence comes to mind: "And the cattle lying on the ground seem to have great and tranquil thoughts." As a matter of fact, I suppose no more vacant mind could be found in the universe than that of the cow when she is reposing in a field chewing her cud. But she is the cause of tranquil if not of great thoughts in the lookers-on, and that is enough. Tranquillity attends her wherever she goes; it beams from her eyes, and lingers in her footsteps.

I sympathize with Whitman as he expressed himself in these lines:—

"I think I could turn and live with the animals, they are
    so placid and self-contain'd.
I stand and look at them, long and long.

"They do not sweat and whine about their condition,
They do not lie awake in the dark and weep for their sins,
They do not make me sick discussing their duty to God.
Not one is dissatisfied, not one is demented with the mania
    of owning things,
Not one kneels to another, nor to his kind that lived
    thousands of years ago,
Not one is respectable or happy over the whole earth."

III

If one has a bit of the farmer in him, it is a pleasure in the
country to have a real farmer for a neighbor—a man whose
heart is in his work, who is not longing for the town or the
city, who improves his fields, who makes two spears of grass
grow where none grew before, whose whole farm has an atmosphere of thrift and well-being. There are so many reluctant,
half-hearted farmers in our Eastern States nowadays, so many
who do only what they have to do in order to survive; who leave
the paternal acres to run to weeds or brush; the paternal fences
to fall into ruins; the paternal orchards untrimmed and un-
ploughed; the paternal meadows unfertilized, while the fertil-
izer wastes in the barnyard; who get but one spear of grass
where their fathers or grandfathers got two or three; and whose
plaint always is that farming does not pay. What is the matter
with our rural population? Has all the good farming blood gone
West, and do only the dregs of it remain?

It is the man who makes the farm, as truly as it is the man who makes any other business; it is the man behind the plough, as truly as it is the man behind the gun, that wins the battle. A half-heart never won a whole sheaf yet. The average farmer has deteriorated. He may know more, but he does less, than his father. He is like the second or third steeping of the tea. Did the original settlers and improvers of the farms, and the generations that followed them, leave all their virtue and grip in the soil? It is certainly true that in my section the last two generations have lived off the capital of labor and brains which their ancestors put into the land; only here and there has a man added anything, only here and there is a farmer who does not wish he had some other business. If such men had that other business, they would reap the same poor results. In the long run, you cannot reap where you have not sown, and the only seed you can sow, in any business that yields tenfold, is yourself—your own wit, your own industry. Unless you plant your heart with your corn, it will mostly go to suckers; unless you strike your own roots into the subsoil of your lands, it will not bear fruit in your character, or in your bank account—all of which is simply saying that thin, leachy land will not bear good crops, and unless a man has the real farming stuff in him, his farm quickly shows it.

My neighbor makes smooth the way of the plough and of the mower. Last summer I saw him take enough stones and rocks from a three-acre field to build quite a fortress; and land whose slumbers had never been disturbed with the plough was soon knee-high with Hungarian grass. How one likes to see a permanent betterment of the land like that!—piles of renegade stone and rock. It is such things that make the country richer. If all New England and New York had had such drastic treatment years ago, the blight of discouraged farming never would have fallen upon them, and the prairie States would not have so far distanced the granite States. A granite soil should grow a better crop of men than the silt of lake or river-bottom, though it yields less corn to the acre.

The prairie makes a strong appeal to a man's indolence and cupidity; it is a place where he can sit at ease and let his team do most of his work. But I much doubt whether the Western farms ever will lay the strong hands upon their possessors that our more varied and picturesque Eastern farms lay. Every field in these farms has a character of its own, and the farms differ from one another as much as the people do. An Eastern farm is the place for a home; the Western farm is the place to grow wheat, pork, and beef. Oh, the flat, featureless, monotonous, cornstalk-littered Middle West! how can the rural virtues of contentment and domesticity thrive there? There is no spot to make your nest except right out on the rim of the world; no spot for a walk or a picnic except in the featureless open of a thousand miles of black prairie—the roads black, straight lines of mud or dust through the landscape; the streams slow, indolent channels of muddy water; the woods, where there are woods, a dull assemblage of straight-trunked trees; the sky a brazen dome that shuts down upon you; there are no hills or mountains to lift it up. The prairie draws no strong distinct lines against the sky; the horizon is vague and baffling. Ah, my mountains are very old measured by the geologic calendar! Yet how foreign to our experience or ways of thinking it seems to speak of mountains as either old or young, as if birth and death applied to them also. But such is the fact: mountains have their day, which day is the geologist's day of millions of years. My mountains were being carved out of a great plateau by the elements while the prairies were still under the sea, and while most of the Rocky Mountains and the Alps and the Himalayas were gestating in the vast earth-womb. In point of age, these mountains beside the Catskills are like infants beside their great-grandfathers. Yet it is a singular contradiction that in their outlines old mountains look young, and young mountains look old. The only youthful feature about young mountains is that they carry their heads very high, and the only old feature about old mountains is that they have a look of repose and calmness and peace. All the gauntness, leanness, angularity, and crumbling decrepitude are with the young mountains; all the smoothness, plumpness, graceful, flowing lines of youth are with the old mountains. Not till the rocks are clothed with soil made out of their own decay are outlines softened and life made possible. Youthful mountains like the Alps are battle-marked by the elements, and their proud heads are continually being laid low by frost, wind, and snow; they are scarred and broken by avalanches the season through. Old mountains, such as the Appalachian System, wear an armor of soil and verdure over their rounded forms on which the arrows of Time have little effect. The turbulent and noisy and stiff-necked period of youth is far behind them.

Hundreds of dairy-farms nestle in the laps of the Catskills; and their huge, grassy aprons, only a little wrinkled here and there, hold as many grazing herds. Woodchuck Lodge is well upon the knee of one of the ranges, and the fields we look upon are like green drapery lying in graceful curves and broad, smooth masses over huge extended limbs. Patches of maple forest here and there bend over a rounded arm or shoulder, like a fur cape upon a woman. Here and there also huge, weather-worn boulders rest upon the ground, dropped there by the moving ice-sheet tens upon tens of thousands of years ago; and here and there are streaks of land completely covered with smaller rocks wedged and driven into the ground. It used to be told me in my youth that the devil's apron-string broke as he was carrying a load of these rocks overhead, and let the mass down upon the ground. The farmers seldom attempt to clear away these leavings of the devil.

IV

My interest in the birds is not as keen as it once was, but they are still an asset in my life. I must live where I can hear the crows caw, the robins sing, and the song sparrow trill. If I can hear also the partridge drum, and the owl hoot, and the chipmunk cluck in the still days of autumn, so much the better. The crow is such a true countryman, so much at home everywhere, so thoroughly in possession of the land, going his way winter and summer in such noisy contentment and pride of possession, that I cannot leave him out. The bird I missed most in California was the crow. I missed his glistening coat in the fields, his ebony form and hearty call in the sky.

One advantage of sleeping out of doors, as we do at Woodchuck Lodge, is that you hear the day ushered in by the birds. Toward autumn you hear the crows first, making proclamation in all directions that it is time to be up and doing, and that life is a good thing. There is not a bit of doubt or discouragement in their tones. They have enjoyed the night, and they have a stout heart for the day. They proclaim it as they fly over my porch at five o'clock in the morning; they call it from the orchard, they bandy the message back and forth in the neighboring fields; the air is streaked with cheery greetings and

raucous salutations. Toward the end of August, or in early
September, I witness with pleasure their huge mass meetings
or annual congress on the pasture hills or in the borders of the
woods. Before that time, you see them singly or in loose bands;
but on some day in late summer, or in early autumn, you see
the clans assemble as if for some rare festival and grand tribal
discussion. A multitudinous cawing attracts your attention,
when you look hillward and see a swarm of dusky forms circling
in the air, their voices mingling in one dissonant wave of sound,
while loose bands of other dusky forms come from all points
of the compass to join them. Presently many hundred crows
are assembled, alternately lighted upon the ground and silently
walking about as if feeding, or circling in the air, cawing as
if they would be heard in the next township. What they are
doing or saying or settling, what it all means, whether they
meet by appointment in the human fashion, whether it is a
jubilee, a parliament, or a convention, I confess I should like
to know. But second thought tells me it is more likely the
gregarious instinct asserting itself after the scatterings and
separations of the summer. The time of the rookery is not far
off, when the inclement season will find all the crows from a
large section of the country massed at night in lonely tree-tops
in some secluded wood.

These early noisy assemblages may be preliminary to the
winter union of the tribe. What an engrossing affair it seems
to be with the crows! how oblivious they appear to all else in
the world! The world was made for crows, and what concerns
them is alone important. The meeting adjourns, from time to
time, from the fields to the woods, then back again, the Babel
of voices waxing or waning according as they are on the wing
or at rest. Sometimes they meet several days in succession and

then disperse, going away in different directions and irregularly, singly or in pairs and bands, as men do on similar occasions. No doubt in these great reunions the crows experience some sort of feeling or emotion, though one would doubtless err in ascribing to them anything like human procedure. It is not a definite purpose, but a tribal instinct, that finds expression in their jubilees.

The crows seem to have a great deal of business besides getting a living. How social, how communicative they are! what picnics they have in the fields and woods, how absolutely at home they are at all times and places! I see them from my window flying by, by twos or threes or more, on happy, holiday wings, sliding down the air, or diving and chasing one another, or walking about the fields, their coats glistening in the sun, the movement of their heads timing the movements of their feet—what an air of independence and respectability and well-being attends them always! The pedestrian crow! No more graceful walker ever trod the turf. How different his bearing from that of a game-bird, and from any of the falcon tribe! He never tries to hide like the former, never morose and sulky like the latter. He is gay and social and in possession of the land; the world is his and he knows it, and life is good.

I suppose that if his flesh were edible, like that of the gallinaceous birds, he would have many more enemies and his whole demeanor would be different. His complacent, self-satisfied air would vanish. He would not advertise his comings and goings so loudly. He would be less conspicuous in the landscape; his huge mass-meetings in September would be more silent and withdrawn. Well, then, he would not be the crow—the happy, devil-may-care creature as we now know him.

His little gayly dressed brother, the jay, does not tempt the sportsman any more than the crow does, but he tempts other creatures—the owl and squirrel, maybe the hawk. Hence his tribe is much less. His range is also more restricted, and his feeding habits much less miscellaneous. Only the woods and groves are his; the fields and rivers he knows not.

The crow is a noisy bird. All his tribe are noisy, but the noise probably has little psychic significance. The raven in Alaska appears to soliloquize most of the time. This talkativeness of the crow tribe is probably only a phase of crow life, and signifies no more and no less than other phases—their color, their cunning, the flick of their wings, and the like. The barnyard fowls are loquacious also, but probably their loquacity is not attended with much psychic activity.

In the mornings of early summer the out-of-door sleeper is more likely to be awakened by the songbirds. In June and early July they strike up about half-past three. "When it is light enough to see that all is well around you, it is light enough to sing," they carol. "Before the early worm is stirring, we will celebrate the coming of day." During the summer the songsparrows have been the first to nudge me in the morning with their songs. One little sparrow in particular would perch on the telephone-wire above the roadside and go through his repertoire of five songs with great regularity and joyousness. He will long be associated in my mind with those early, fragrant, summer dawns. One of his five songs fell so easily into words that I had only to call the attention of my friends to it to have them hear the words that I heard, "If, if, if you please, Mr. Durkee,"—the last word a little prolonged, and with a rising inflection. Another was not quite so well expressed by these words: "Please, please, speak to me, sweetheart." The third one suggested this sentence: "Then, then, Fitzhugh says, yes, sir!" The fourth one was something like this: "If, if, if you seize her, do it quick." The fifth one baffled me to suggest by words. But in August his musical enthusiasm began to decline. His different songs lost their distinctiveness and emphasis. It was as if they had faded and become blurred with the progress of the season.

The little birds are insignificant and unobtrusive on the great background of nature, yet if one learns to distinguish them and to love them, their songs may become a sort of accompaniment to one's daily life. Last May, while I was much occupied in repairing and making habitable my old farmhouse, a solitary mourning ground-warbler, which one rarely sees or hears, came and tarried about the place for a week or ten days, singing most of each forenoon in the orchard and garden about the house, and giving to my occupation a touch of something rare and sylvan. He lent to the old apple-trees, which I had known as a boy, an interest that the boy knew not. Then he went away, whether on the arrival of his mate or not I do not know.

A butternut-tree stands across the road in front of Wood-chuck Lodge. One season the red squirrels stored the butter-nuts in the wall of one of the upper rooms of the unoccupied house, to which they gained access through a hole in the siding. When we moved in, in the summer, the squirrels soon became uneasy, and one day one of them began removing the butter-nuts, not to some other granary or place of safety, but to the grass and dry leaves on the ground in the orchard. He was unwittingly planting them by the act of hiding them. The au-tomatic character of much animal behavior, the extent to which their lives flow in fixed channels, was well seen in the behavior of this squirrel. His procedure in transferring the nuts from his den in the house to the ground in the orchard, a distance of probably one hundred feet, was as definite and regular as the movement of a piece of machinery. He would rush up and over the roof of the house with a nut in his mouth, by those sharp, spasmodic sallies so characteristic of the movements of the red squirrel, down the corner of the house to the ground by the same jerky movements, across some rubbish and open ground in the same manner, alert and cautious, up the corner of a small building ten feet high and eight long, over its roof, with arched tail and spread feet, snickering and jerking, down to the ground on the other side, dashing to the trunk of an apple-tree ten feet away, up it a few feet to make an observation, then down to the ground again, and out into the grass, where he would carefully hide his nut, and cover it with leaves. Then back to the house again he would go by precisely the same route and with precisely the same movements, and bring another nut. Day after day I saw him thus engaged till apparently all the nuts were removed. He probably did not know he was planting butternut-trees for other red squirrels, but that was what he was doing. The crows and jays carry away and plant acorns and chestnuts in the same way, thus often causing a pine forest to be succeeded by these trees.

The red squirrel is only an irregular storer of nuts in the autumn. In this respect he stands halfway between the chipmunk and the gray squirrel, one of which regularly lays up winter stores and the other none at all.*

How diverse are the ways of nature in reaching the same end! Both the chipmunk and the woodchuck lay up stores

---

* The gray squirrel hides nuts under the leaves and grass but he lays up no winter stores.

against the needs of winter, the latter in the shape of fat upon his own ribs, and the former in the shape of seeds and nuts in his den in the ground; and I fancy that one of them is no more conscious of what he is doing than the other. Animals do not take conscious thought of the future; it is as if something in their organization took thought for them. One November, seized with the cruel desire to go to the bottom of the question of the chipmunk's winter stores, I dug out one after he had got his house settled for the season. I found his den three feet below the surface of the ground—just beyond the frost-line— and containing nearly four quarts of various seeds, most of them the little black grains of wild buckwheat—two hundred and fifty thousand of them, I estimated—all cleaned of their husks as neatly as if done by some patent machinery.

How many perilous journeys along stone walls and through weedy tangles this store of seeds represented! One would say at least a thousand trips, beset by many dangers from hawks and cats and weasels and other enemies of the little rodent.

The chipmunk is provident; he is a wise housekeeper, but one can hardly envy him those three or four months of inaction in the pitchy darkness of his subterranean den. His mate is not with him, and evidently the oblivion of the hibernating sleep, like that of the woodchuck and of certain mice, is not his. The life of the red and gray squirrels, who are more or less active all winter, seems preferable. They lay up no stores and are no doubt often cold and hungry, but the light of day and the freedom of the snow and of the tree-tops are theirs. Abundant stores are a good thing for both man and beast, but action, adventure, struggle are better.

SPECKLED
TROUT

I

The legend of the wary trout, hinted at in the last sketch,* is to be further illustrated in this and some following chapters. We shall get at more of the meaning of those dark water-lines, and I hope, also, not entirely miss the significance of the gold and silver spots and the glancing iridescent hues. The trout is dark and obscure above, but behind this foil there are wondrous tints that reward the believing eye. Those who seek him in his wild remote haunts are quite sure to get the full force of the sombre and uninviting aspects, —the wet, the cold, the toil, the broken rest, and the huge, savage, uncompromising nature, etc.,—but the true angler sees farther than these, and is never thwarted of his legitimate reward by them.

I have been a seeker of trout from my boyhood, and on all the expeditions in which this fish has been the ostensible purpose I have brought home more game than my creel showed.

* In the Wake-Robin edition of *The Complete Writings of John Burroughs*, vol. 3: *Locusts and Wild Honey* (1924), "Speckled Trout" is preceded by Burroughs's essay "Is It Going to Rain?"

In fact, in my mature years I find I got more of nature into me, more of the woods, the wild, nearer to bird and beast, while threading my native streams for trout, than in almost any other way. It furnished a good excuse to go forth; it pitched one in the right key; it sent one through the fat and marrowy places of field and wood. Then the fisherman has a harmless, preoccupied look; he is a kind of vagrant that nothing fears. He blends himself with the trees and the shadows. All his approaches are gentle and indirect. He times himself to the meandering, soliloquizing stream; its impulse bears him along. At the foot of the waterfall he sits sequestered and hidden in its volume of sound. The birds know he has no designs upon them, and the animals see that his mind is in the creek. His enthusiasm anneals him and makes him pliable to the scenes and influences he moves among.

Then what acquaintance he makes with the stream! He addresses himself to it as a lover to his mistress; he wooes it and stays with it till he knows its most hidden secrets. It runs through his thoughts not less than through its banks there; he feels the fret and thrust of every bar and bowlder. Where it deepens, his purpose deepens; where it is shallow he is indifferent. He knows how to interpret its every glance and dimple; its beauty haunts him for days.

I am sure I run no risk of overpraising the charm and attractiveness of a well-fed trout stream, every drop of water in it as bright and pure as if the nymphs had brought it all the way from its source in crystal goblets, and as cool as if it had been hatched beneath a glacier. When the heated and soiled and jaded refugee from the city first sees one, he feels as if he would like to turn it into his bosom and let it flow through him a few hours, it suggests such healing freshness and newness. How his roily thoughts would run clear; how the sediment would go down-stream! Could he ever have an impure or an unwholesome wish afterward? The next best thing he can do is to tramp along its banks and surrender himself to its influence. If he reads it intently enough, he will, in a measure, be taking it into his mind and heart, and experiencing its salutary ministrations.

Trout streams coursed through every valley my boyhood knew. I crossed them, and was often lured and detained by them, on my way to and from school. We bathed in them during the long summer noons, and felt for the trout under their banks. A holiday was a holiday indeed that brought permission to go fishing over on Rose's Brook, or up Hardscrabble, or in Meeker's Hollow; all-day trips, from morning till night, through meadows and pastures and beechen woods, wherever the shy, limpid stream led. What an appetite it developed! a hunger that was fierce and aboriginal, and that the wild strawberries we plucked as we crossed the hill teased rather than allayed. When but a few hours could be had, gained perhaps by doing some piece of work about the farm or garden in half the allotted time, the little creek that headed in the paternal domain was handy; when half a day was at one's disposal, there were the hemlocks, less than a mile distant, with their loitering, meditative, log-impeded stream and their dusky, fragrant depths. Alert and wide-eyed, one picked his way along, startled now and then by the sudden bursting-up of the partridge, or by the whistling wings of the "dropping snipe," pressing through the brush and the briers, or finding an easy passage over the trunk of a prostrate tree, carefully letting his hook down through some tangle into a still pool, or standing in some high sombre avenue and watching his line float in and out amid the moss-covered bowlders. In my first essayings I used to go to the edge of these hemlocks, seldom dipping into them beyond the first pool where the stream swept under the roots of two large trees. From this point I could look back into the sunlit fields where the cattle were grazing; beyond, all was gloom and mystery; the trout were black, and to my young imagination the silence and the shadows were blacker. But gradually I yielded to the fascination and penetrated the woods farther and farther on each expedition, till the heart of the mystery was fairly plucked out. During the second or third year of my piscatorial experience I went through them, and through the pasture and meadow beyond, and through another strip of hemlocks, to where the little stream joined the main creek of the valley.

In June, when my trout fever ran pretty high, and an auspicious day arrived, I would make a trip to a stream a couple of miles distant, that came down out of a comparatively new settlement. It was a rapid mountain brook presenting many difficult problems to the young angler, but a very enticing stream for all that, with its two saw-mill dams, its pretty cascades, its high, shelving rocks sheltering the mossy nests of the phœbe-bird, and its general wild and forbidding aspects.

But a meadow brook was always a favorite. The trout like meadows; doubtless their food is more abundant there, and, usually, the good hiding-places are more numerous. As soon as you strike a meadow the character of the creek changes: it goes slower and lies deeper; it tarries to enjoy the high, cool banks and to half hide beneath them; it loves the willows, or rather the willows love it and shelter it from the sun; its spring runs are kept cool by the overhanging grass, and the heavy turf that faces its open banks is not cut away by the sharp hoofs of the grazing cattle. Then there are the bobolinks and starlings and meadowlarks, always interested spectators of the angler; there are also the marsh marigolds, the buttercups, or the spotted lilies, and the good angler is always an interested spectator of them. In fact, the patches of meadow land that lie in the angler's course are like the happy experiences in his own life, or like the fine passages in the poem he is reading; the pasture oftener contains the shallow and monotonous places. In the small streams the cattle scare the fish, and soil their element and break down their retreats under the banks. Woodland alternates the best with meadow: the creek loves to burrow under the roots of a great tree, to scoop out a pool after leaping over the prostrate trunk of one, and to pause at the foot of a ledge of moss-covered rocks, with ice-cold water dripping down. How straight the current goes for the rock! Note its corrugated, muscular appearance; it strikes and glances off, but accumulates, deepens with well-defined eddies above and to one side; on the edge of these the trout lurk and spring upon their prey.

The angler learns that it is generally some obstacle or hindrance that makes a deep place in the creek, as in a brave life; and his ideal brook is one that lies in deep, well-defined banks, yet makes many a shift from right to left, meets with many rebuffs and adventures, hurled back upon itself by rocks, waylaid by snags and trees, tripped up by precipices, but sooner or later reposing under meadow banks, deepening and eddying beneath bridges, or prosperous and strong in some level stretch of cultivated land with great elms shading it here and there.

But I early learned that from almost any stream in a trout country the true angler could take trout, and that the great secret was this, that, whatever bait you used, worm, grass-hopper, grub, or fly, there was one thing you must always put upon your hook, namely, your heart: when you bait your hook with your heart the fish always bite; they will jump clear from the water after it; they will dispute with each other over it; it is a morsel they love above everything else. With such bait I have seen the born angler (my grandfather was one) take a noble string of trout from the most unpromising waters, and on the most unpromising day. He used his hook so coyly and tenderly, he approached the fish with such address and insin-uation, he divined the exact spot where they lay: if they were not eager he humored them and seemed to steal by them; if they were playful and coquettish he would suit his mood to theirs; if they were frank and sincere he met them half way; he was so patient and considerate, so entirely devoted to pleas-ing the critical trout, and so successful in his efforts,—surely his heart was upon his hook, and it was a tender, unctuous heart, too, as that of every angler is. How nicely he would measure the distance! how dexterously he would avoid an over-hanging limb or bush and drop the line exactly in the right spot! Of course there was a pulse of feeling and sympathy to the extremity of that line. If your heart is a stone, however, or an empty husk, there is no use to put it upon your hook; it will not tempt the fish; the bait must be quick and fresh. Indeed, a certain quality of youth is indispensable to the suc-cessful angler, a certain unworldliness and readiness to invest yourself in an enterprise that doesn't pay in the current coin. Not only is the angler, like the poet, born and not made, as Walton says, but there is a deal of the poet in him, and he is to be judged no more harshly; he is the victim of his genius: those wild streams, how they haunt him! he will play truant to dull care, and flee to them; their waters impart somewhat of their own perpetual youth to him. My grandfather when he was eighty years old would take down his pole as eagerly as any boy, and step off with wonderful elasticity toward the beloved streams; it used to try my young legs a good deal to follow him, specially on the return trip. And no poet was ever more innocent of worldly success or ambition. For, to paraphrase Tennyson,—

"Lusty trout to him were scrip and share,
And babbling waters more than cent for cent."

He laid up treasures, but they were not in this world. In fact, though the kindest of husbands, I fear he was not what the country people call a "good provider," except in providing trout in their season, though it is doubtful if there was always fat in the house to fry them in. But he could tell you they were worse off than that at Valley Forge, and that trout, or any other fish, were good roasted in the ashes under the coals. He had the Walton requisite of loving quietness and contemplation, and was devout withal. Indeed, in many ways he was akin to those Galilee fishermen who were called to be fishers of men. How he read the Book and pored over it, even at times, I suspect, nodding over it, and laying it down only to take up his rod, over which, unless the trout were very dilatory and the journey very fatiguing, he never nodded!

II

The Delaware is one of our minor rivers, but it is a stream beloved of the trout. Nearly all its remote branches head in mountain springs, and its collected waters, even when warmed by the summer sun, are as sweet and wholesome as dew swept from the grass. The Hudson wins from it two streams that are fathered by the mountains from whose loins most of its beginnings issue, namely, the Rondout and the Esopus. These swell a more illustrious current than the Delaware, but the Rondout, one of the finest trout streams in the world, makes an uncanny alliance before it reaches its destination, namely, with the malarious Wallkill.

In the same nest of mountains from which they start are born the Neversink and the Beaverkill, streams of wondrous beauty that flow south and west into the Delaware. From my native hills I could catch glimpses of the mountains in whose laps these creeks were cradled, but it was not till after many years, and after dwelling in a country where trout are not found, that I returned to pay my respects to them as an angler.

My first acquaintance with the Neversink was made in company with some friends in 1869. We passed up the valley of the Big Ingin, marveling at its copious ice-cold springs, and its immense sweep of heavy-timbered mountain sides. Crossing the range at its head, we struck the Neversink quite unexpectedly about the middle of the afternoon, at a point where it was a good-sized trout stream. It proved to be one of those black mountain brooks born of innumerable ice-cold springs, nourished in the shade, and shod, as it were, with thick-matted moss, that every camper-out remembers. The fish are as black as the stream and very wild. They dart from beneath the fringed rocks, or dive with the hook into the dusky depths,—an integral part of the silence and the shadows. The spell of the moss is over all. The fisherman's tread is noiseless, as he leaps from stone to stone and from ledge to ledge along the bed of the stream. How cool it is! He looks up the dark, silent defile, hears the solitary voice of the water, sees the decayed trunks of fallen trees bridging the stream, and all he has dreamed, when a boy, of the haunts of beasts of prey—the crouching feline tribes, especially if it be near nightfall and the gloom already deepening in the woods—comes freshly to mind, and he presses on, wary and alert, and speaking to his companions in low tones.

After an hour or so the trout became less abundant, and with nearly a hundred of the black sprites in our baskets we turned back. Here and there I saw the abandoned nests of the pigeons, sometimes half a dozen in one tree. In a yellow birch which the floods had uprooted, a number of nests were still in place, little shelves or platforms of twigs loosely arranged, and affording little or no protection to the eggs or the young birds against inclement weather.

Before we had reached our companions the rain set in again and forced us to take shelter under a balsam. When it slackened we moved on and soon came up with Aaron, who had caught his first trout, and, considerably drenched, was making his way toward camp, which one of the party had gone forward to build. After traveling less than a mile, we saw a smoke struggling up through the dripping trees, and in a few moments were all standing round a blazing fire. But the rain now commenced again, and fairly poured down through the trees, rendering the prospect of cooking and eating our supper there in the woods, and of passing the night on the ground without tent or cover of any kind, rather disheartening. We had been told of a bark shanty a couple of miles farther down the creek, and thitherward we speedily took up our line of march. When we were on the point of discontinuing the search, thinking we had been misinformed or had passed it by, we came in sight of a barkpeeling, in the midst of which a small log house lifted its naked rafters toward the now breaking sky. It had neither floor nor roof, and was less inviting on first sight than the open woods. But a board partition was still standing, out of which we built a rude porch on the east side of the house, large enough for us all to sleep under if well packed, and eat under if we stood up. There was plenty of well-seasoned timber lying about, and a fire was soon burning in front of our quarters that made the scene social and picturesque, especially when the frying-pans were brought into requisition, and the coffee, in charge of Aaron, who was an artist in this line, mingled its aroma with the wild-wood air. At dusk a balsam was felled, and the tips of the branches used to make a bed, which was more fragrant than soft; hemlock is better, because its needles are finer and its branches more elastic.

There was a spirt or two of rain during the night, but not enough to find out the leaks in our roof. It took the shower or series of showers of the next day to do that. They commenced about two o'clock in the afternoon. The forenoon had been fine, and we had brought into camp nearly three hundred trout; but before they were half dressed, or the first panfuls fried, the rain set in. First came short, sharp dashes, then a gleam of treacherous sunshine, followed by more and heavier dashes. The wind was in the southwest, and to rain seemed the easiest thing in the world. From fitful dashes to a steady pour the transition was natural. We stood huddled together, stark and grim, under our cover, like hens under a cart. The fire fought bravely for a time, and retaliated with sparks and spiteful tongues of flame; but gradually its spirit was broken, only a heavy body of coal and half-consumed logs in the centre holding out against all odds. The simmering fish were soon floating about in a yellow liquid that did not look in the least appetizing. Point after point gave way in our cover, till standing between the drops was no longer possible. The water coursed down the underside of the boards, and dripped in our necks and formed puddles on our hat-brims. We shifted our guns and traps and viands, till there was no longer any choice of position, when the loaves and the fishes, the salt and the sugar, the pork and the butter, shared the same watery fate. The fire was gasping its last. Little rivulets coursed about it, and bore away the quenched but steaming coals on their bosoms. The spring run in the rear of our camp swelled so rapidly that part of the trout that had been hastily left lying on its banks again found themselves quite at home. For over two hours the floods came down. About four o'clock Orville, who had not yet come from the day's sport, appeared. To say Orville was wet is not much; he was better than that,—he had been washed and rinsed in at least half a dozen waters, and the trout that he bore dangling at the end of a string hardly knew that they had been out of their proper element.

But he brought welcome news. He had been two or three miles down the creek, and had seen a log building,—whether house or stable he did not know, but it had the appearance of having a good roof, which was inducement enough for us instantly to leave our present quarters. Our course lay along an old wood-road, and much of the time we were to our knees in water. The woods were literally flooded everywhere. Every little rill and springlet ran like a mill-tail, while the main stream rushed and roared, foaming, leaping, lashing, its volume increased fifty fold. The water was not roily, but of a rich coffee-color, from the leachings of the woods. No more trout for the next three days! we thought as we looked upon the rampant stream.

After we had labored and floundered along for about an hour, the road turned to the left, and in a little stumpy clearing near the creek a gable uprose on our view. It did not prove to be just such a place as poets love to contemplate. It required a greater effort of the imagination than any of us were then capable of to believe it had ever been a favorite resort of wood-nymphs or sylvan deities. It savored rather of the equine and the bovine. The bark-men had kept their teams there, horses on the one side and oxen on the other, and no Hercules had ever done duty in cleansing the stables. But there was a dry loft overhead with some straw, where we might get some sleep, in spite of the rain and the midges; a double layer of boards, standing at a very acute angle, would keep off the former, while the mingled refuse hay and muck beneath would nurse a smoke that would prove a thorough protection against the latter. And then, when Jim, the two-handed, mounting the trunk of a prostrate maple near by, had severed it thrice with easy and familiar stroke, and, rolling the logs in front of the shanty, had kindled a fire, which, getting the better of the dampness, soon cast a bright glow over all, shedding warmth and light even into the dingy stable, I consented to unsling my knapsack and accept the situation. The rain had ceased and the sun shone out behind the woods. We had trout sufficient for present needs; and after my first meal in an ox-stall, I strolled out on the rude log bridge to watch the angry Neversink rush by. Its waters fell quite as rapidly as they rose, and before sundown it looked as if we might have fishing again on the morrow. We had better sleep that night than either night before, though there were two disturbing causes,—the smoke in the early part of it, and the cold in the latter. The "no-see-ems" left in disgust; and, though disgusted myself, I swallowed the smoke as best I could, and hugged my pallet of straw the closer. But the day dawned bright, and a plunge in the Never-sink set me all right again. The creek, to our surprise and gratification, was only a little higher than before the rain, and some of the finest trout we had yet seen we caught that morning near camp.

We tarried yet another day and night at the old stable, but taking our meals outside squatted on the ground, which had now become quite dry. Part of the day I spent strolling about the woods, looking up old acquaintances among the birds, and, as always, half expectant of making some new ones. Curiously enough, the most abundant species were among those I had found rare in most other localities, namely, the small water-wagtail, the mourning ground warbler, and the yellow-bellied woodpecker. The latter seems to be the prevailing woodpecker through the woods of this region.

That night the midges, those motes that sting, held high carnival. We learned afterward, in the settlement below and from the barkpeelers, that it was the worst night ever experienced in that valley. We had done no fishing during the day, but had anticipated some fine sport about sundown. Accordingly Aaron and I started off between six and seven o'clock, one going up stream and the other down. The scene was charming. The sun shot up great spokes of light from behind the woods, and beauty, like a presence, pervaded the atmosphere. But torment, multiplied as the sands of the seashore, lurked in every tangle and thicket. In a thoughtless moment I removed my shoes and socks, and waded in the water to secure a fine trout that had accidentally slipped from my string and was helplessly floating with the current. This caused some delay and gave the gnats time to accumulate. Before I had got one foot half dressed I was enveloped in a black mist that settled upon my hands and neck and face, filling my ears with infinitesimal bitings. I thought I should have to flee to the friendly fumes of the old stable, with "one stocking off and one stocking on"; but I got my shoe on at last, though not without many amusing interruptions and digressions.

In a few moments after this adventure I was in rapid retreat toward camp. Just as I reached the path leading from the shanty to the creek, my companion in the same ignoble flight reached it also, his hat broken and rumpled, and his sanguine countenance looking more sanguinary than I had ever before seen it, and his speech, also, in the highest degree inflammatory. His face and forehead were as blotched and swollen as if he had just run his head into a hornets' nest, and his manner as precipitate as if the whole swarm was still at his back.

No smoke or smudge which we ourselves could endure was sufficient in the earlier part of that evening to prevent serious annoyance from the same cause; but later a respite was granted us.

About ten o'clock, as we stood round our campfire, we were startled by a brief but striking display of the aurora borealis. My imagination had already been excited by talk of legends and of weird shapes and appearances, and when, on looking up toward the sky, I saw those pale, phantasmal waves of magnetic light chasing each other across the little opening above our heads, and at first sight seeming barely to clear the treetops, I was as vividly impressed as if I had caught a glimpse of a veritable spectre of the Neversink. The sky shook and trembled like a great white curtain.

After we had climbed to our loft and had lain down to sleep, another adventure befell us. This time a new and un-inviting customer appeared upon the scene, the *genius loci* of the old stable, namely, the "fretful porcupine." We had seen the marks and work of these animals about the shanty, and had been careful each night to hang our traps, guns, etc., beyond their reach, but of the prickly night-walker himself we feared we should not get a view.

We had lain down some half hour, and I was just on the threshold of sleep, ready, as it were, to pass through the open door into the land of dreams, when I heard outside somewhere that curious sound,—a sound which I had heard every night I spent in these woods, not only on this but on former expe-ditions, and which I had settled in my mind as proceeding from the porcupine, since I knew the sounds our other common animals were likely to make,—a sound that might be either a gnawing on some hard, dry substance, or a grating of teeth, or a shrill grunting.

Orville heard it also, and, raising up on his elbow, asked, "What is that?"

"What the hunters call a 'porcupig,' " said I.

"Sure?"

"Entirely so."

"Why does he make that noise?"

"It is a way he has of cursing our fire," I replied. "I heard him last night also."

"Where do you suppose he is?" inquired my companion, showing a disposition to look him up.

"Not far off, perhaps fifteen or twenty yards from our fire, where the shadows begin to deepen."

Orville slipped into his trousers, felt for my gun, and in a moment had disappeared down through the scuttle hole. I had no disposition to follow him, but was rather annoyed than otherwise at the disturbance. Getting the direction of the sound, he went picking his way over the rough, uneven ground, and, when he got where the light failed him, poking every doubtful object with the end of his gun. Presently he poked a light grayish object, like a large round stone, which surprised him by moving off. On this hint he fired, making an incurable wound in the "porcupig," which, nevertheless, tried harder than ever to escape. I lay listening, when, close on the heels of the report of the gun, came excited shouts for a revolver. Snatching up my Smith and Wesson, I hastened, shoeless and hatless, to the scene of action, wondering what was up. I found my companion struggling to detain, with the end of the gun, an uncertain object that was trying to crawl off into the darkness. "Look out!" said Orville, as he saw my bare feet, "the quills are lying thick around here."

And so they were; he had blown or beaten them nearly all off the poor creature's back, and was in a fair way completely to disable my gun, the ramrod of which was already broken and splintered clubbing his victim. But a couple of shots from the revolver, sighted by a lighted match, at the head of the animal, quickly settled him.

It proved to be an unusually large Canada porcupine,— an old patriarch, gray and venerable, with spines three inches long, and weighing, I should say, twenty pounds. The build of this animal is much like that of the woodchuck, that is, heavy and pouchy. The nose is blunter than that of the woodchuck, the limbs stronger, and the tail broader and heavier. Indeed, the latter appendage is quite club-like, and the animal can, no doubt, deal a smart blow with it. An old hunter with whom I talked thought it aided them in climbing. They are inveterate gnawers, and spend much of their time in trees gnawing the bark. In winter one will take up its abode in a hemlock, and continue there till the tree is quite denuded. The carcass emitted a peculiar offensive odor, and, though very fat, was not in the least inviting as game. If it is part of the economy of nature for one animal to prey upon some other beneath it, then the poor devil has indeed a mouthful that makes a meal off the porcupine. Panthers and lynxes have essayed it, but have invariably left off at the first course, and have afterwards been found dead, or nearly so, with their heads puffed up like a pincushion, and the quills protruding on all sides. A dog that understands the business will manœuvre round the porcupine till he gets an opportunity to throw it over on its back, when he fastens on its quilless underbody. Aaron was puzzled to know how long-parted friends could embrace, when it was suggested that the quills could be depressed or elevated at pleasure.

The next morning boded rain; but we had become thoroughly sated with the delights of our present quarters, outside and in, and packed up our traps to leave. Before we had reached the clearing, three miles below, the rain set in, keeping up a lazy, monotonous drizzle till the afternoon.

The clearing was quite a recent one, made mostly by barkpeelers, who followed their calling in the mountains round about in summer, and worked in their shops making shingle in winter. The Biscuit Brook came in here from the west,—a fine, rapid trout stream six or eight miles in length, with plenty of deer in the mountains about its head. On its banks we found the house of an old woodman, to whom we had been directed for information about the section we proposed to traverse.

"Is the way very difficult," we inquired, "across from the Neversink into the head of the Beaverkill?"

"Not to me; I could go it the darkest night ever was. And I can direct you so you can find the way without any trouble. You go down the Neversink about a mile, when you come to Highfall Brook, the first stream that comes down on the right. Follow up it to Jim Reed's shanty, about three miles. Then cross the stream, and on the left bank, pretty well up on the side of the mountain, you will find a wood-road, which was made by a fellow below here who stole some ash logs off the top of the ridge last winter and drew them out on the snow. When the road first begins to tilt over the mountain, strike down to your left, and you can reach the Beaverkill before sundown."

As it was then after two o'clock, and as the distance was six or eight of these terrible hunters' miles, we concluded to take a whole day to it, and wait till next morning. The Beaverkill flowed west, the Neversink south, and I had a mortal dread of getting entangled amid the mountains and valleys that lie in either angle.

Besides, I was glad of another and final opportunity to pay my respects to the finny tribes of the Neversink. At this point it was one of the finest trout streams I had ever beheld. It was so sparkling, its bed so free from sediment or impurities of any kind, that it had a new look, as if it had just come from the hand of its Creator. I tramped along its margin upward of a mile that afternoon, part of the time wading to my knees, and casting my hook, baited only with a trout's fin, to the opposite bank. Trout are real cannibals, and make no bones, and break none either, in lunching on each other. A friend of mine had several in his spring, when one day a large female trout gulped down one of her male friends, nearly one third her own size, and went around for two days with the tail of her liege lord protruding from her mouth! A fish's eye will do for bait, though the anal fin is better. One of the natives here told me that when he wished to catch large trout (and I judged he never fished for any other,—I never do), he used for bait the bullhead, or dart, a little fish an inch and a half or two inches long, that rests on the pebbles near shore and darts quickly, when disturbed, from point to point. "Put that on your hook," said he, "and if there is a big fish in the creek he is bound to have it." But the darts were not easily found; the big fish, I concluded, had cleaned them all out; and, then, it was easy enough to supply our wants with a fin.

Declining the hospitable offers of the settlers, we spread our blankets that night in a dilapidated shingle-shop on the banks of the Biscuit Brook, first flooring the damp ground with the new shingle that lay piled in one corner. The place had a great-throated chimney with a tremendous expanse of fireplace within, that cried "More!" at every morsel of wood we gave it.

But I must hasten over this part of the ground, nor let the delicious flavor of the milk we had that morning for breakfast, and that was so delectable after four days of fish, linger on my tongue; nor yet tarry to set down the talk of that honest, weather-worn passer-by who paused before our door, and every moment on the point of resuming his way, yet stood for an hour and recited his adventures hunting deer and bears on these mountains. Having replenished our stock of bread and salt pork at the house of one of the settlers, midday found us at Reed's shanty,—one of those temporary structures erected by the bark jobber to lodge and board his "hands" near their work. Jim not being at home, we could gain no information from the "women folks" about the way, nor from the men who had just come in to dinner; so we pushed on, as near as we could, according to the instructions we had previously received. Crossing the creek, we forced our way up the side of the mountain, through a perfect *cheval-de-frise* of fallen and peeled hemlocks, and, entering the dense woods above, began to look anxiously about for the wood-road. My companions at first could see no trace of it; but knowing that a casual wood-road cut in winter, when there was likely to be two or three feet of snow on the ground, would present only the slightest indications to the eye in summer, I looked a little closer, and could make out a mark or two here and there. The larger trees had been avoided, and the axe used only on the small saplings and underbrush, which had been lopped off a couple of feet from the ground. By being constantly on the alert, we followed it till near the top of the mountain; but, when looking to see it "tilt" over the other side, it disappeared altogether. Some stumps of the black cherry were found, and a solitary pair of snow-shoes were hanging high and dry on a branch, but no further trace of human hands could we see. While we were resting here a couple of hermit thrushes, one of them with some sad defect in his vocal powers which barred him from uttering more than a few notes of his song, gave voice to the solitude of the place. This was the second instance in which I have observed a song-bird with apparently some organic defect in its instrument. The other case was that of a bobolink, which, hover in midair and inflate its throat as it might, could only force out a few incoherent notes. But the bird in each case presented this striking contrast to human examples of the kind, that it was apparently just as proud of itself, and just as well satisfied with its performance, as its more successful rivals.

After deliberating some time over a pocket compass which I carried, we decided upon our course, and held on to the west. The descent was very gradual. Traces of bear and deer were noted at different points, but not a live animal was seen.

About four o'clock we reached the bank of a stream flowing west. Hail to the Beaverkill! and we pushed on along its banks. The trout were plenty, and rose quickly to the hook; but we held on our way, designing to go into camp about six o'clock. Many inviting places, first on one bank, then on the other, made us linger, till finally we reached a smooth, dry place overshadowed by balsam and hemlock, where the creek bent around a little flat, which was so entirely to our fancy that we unslung our knapsacks at once. While my companions were cutting wood and making other preparations for the night, it fell to my lot, as the most successful angler, to provide the trout for supper and breakfast. How shall I describe that wild, beautiful stream, with features so like those of all other mountain streams? And yet, as I saw it in the deep twilight of those woods on that June afternoon, with its steady, even flow, and its tranquil, many-voiced murmur, it made an impression upon my mind distinct and peculiar, fraught in an eminent degree with the charm of seclusion and remoteness. The solitude was perfect, and I felt that strangeness and insignificance which the civilized man must always feel when opposing himself to such a vast scene of silence and wildness. The trout were quite black, like all wood trout, and took the bait eagerly. I followed the stream till the deepening shadows warned me to turn back.

As I neared camp, the fire shone far through the trees, dispelling the gathering gloom, but blinding my eyes to all obstacles at my feet. I was seriously disturbed on arriving to find that one of my companions had cut an ugly gash in his shin with the axe while felling a tree. As we did not carry a fifth wheel, it was not just the time or place to have any of our members crippled, and I had bodings of evil. But, thanks to the healing virtues of the balsam which must have adhered to the blade of the axe, and double thanks to the court-plaster with which Orville had supplied himself before leaving home, the wounded leg, by being favored that night and the next day, gave us little trouble.

That night we had our first fair and square camping out, —that is, sleeping on the ground with no shelter over us but the trees,—and it was in many respects the pleasantest night we spent in the woods. The weather was perfect and the place was perfect, and for the first time we were exempt from the midges and smoke; and then we appreciated the clean new page we had to work on. Nothing is so acceptable to the camper-out as a pure article in the way of woods and waters. Any admixture of human relics mars the spirit of the scene. Yet I am willing to confess that, before we were through those woods, the marks of an axe in a tree was a welcome sight. On resuming our march next day we followed the right bank of the Beaverkill, in order to strike a stream which flowed in from the north, and which was the outlet of Balsam Lake, the objective point of that day's march. The distance to the lake from our camp could not have been over six or seven miles; yet, traveling as we did, without path or guide, climbing up banks, plunging into ravines, making detours around swampy places, and forcing our way through woods choked up with much fallen and decayed timber, it seemed at least twice that distance, and the mid-afternoon sun was shining when we emerged into what is called the "Quaker Clearing," ground that I had been over nine years before, and that lies about two miles south of the lake. From this point we had a well-worn path that led us up a sharp rise of ground, then through level woods till we saw the bright gleam of the water through the trees.

I am always struck, on approaching these little mountain lakes, with the extensive preparation that is made for them in the conformation of the ground. I am thinking of a depression, or natural basin, in the side of the mountain or on its top, the brink of which I shall reach after a little steep climbing; but instead of that, after I have accomplished the ascent, I find a broad sweep of level or gently undulating woodland that brings me after a half hour or so to the lake, which lies in this vast lap like a drop of water in the palm of a man's hand.

Balsam Lake was oval-shaped, scarcely more than half a mile long and a quarter of a mile wide, but presented a charming picture, with a group of dark gray hemlocks filling the valley about its head, and the mountains rising above and beyond. We found a bough house in good repair, also a dug-out and paddle and several floats of logs. In the dug-out I was soon creeping along the shady side of the lake, where the trout were incessantly jumping for a species of black fly, that, sheltered from the slight breeze, were dancing in swarms just above the surface of the water. The gnats were there in swarms also, and did their best toward balancing the accounts by preying upon me while I preyed upon the trout which preyed upon the flies. But by dint of keeping my hands, face, and neck constantly wet, I am convinced that the balance of blood was on my side. The trout jumped most within a foot or two of shore, where the water was only a few inches deep. The shallowness of the water, perhaps, accounted for the inability of the fish to do more than lift their heads above the surface. They came up mouth wide open, and dropped back again in the most impotent manner. Where there is any depth of water, a trout will jump several feet into the air; and where there is a solid, unbroken sheet or column, they will scale falls and dams fifteen feet high.

We had the very cream and flower of our trout-fishing at this lake. For the first time we could use the fly to advantage; and then the contrast between laborious tramping along shore, on the one hand, and sitting in one end of a dug-out and casting your line right and left with no fear of entanglement in brush or branch, while you were gently propelled along, on the other, was of the most pleasing character.

There were two varieties of trout in the lake,—what it seems proper to call silver trout and golden trout; the former were the slimmer, and seemed to keep apart from the latter. Starting from the outlet and working round on the eastern side toward the head, we invariably caught these first. They glanced in the sun like bars of silver. Their sides and bellies were indeed as white as new silver. As we neared the head, and especially as we came near a space occupied by some kind of watergrass that grew in the deeper part of the lake, the other variety would begin to take the hook, their bellies a bright gold color, which became a deep orange on their fins; and as we returned to the place of departure with the bottom of the boat strewn with these bright forms intermingled, it was a sight not soon to be forgotten. It pleased my eye so, that I would fain linger over them, arranging them in rows and studying the various hues and tints. They were of nearly a uniform size, rarely one over ten or under eight inches in length, and it seemed as if the hues of all the precious metals and stones were reflected from their sides. The flesh was deep salmon-color; that of brook trout is generally much lighter. Some hunters and fishers from the valley of the Mill Brook, whom we met here, told us the trout were much larger in the lake, though far less numerous than they used to be. Brook-trout do not grow large till they become scarce. It is only in streams that have been long and much fished that I have caught them as much as sixteen inches in length.

The "porcupigs" were numerous about the lake, and not at all shy. One night the heat became so intolerable in our oven-shaped bough house that I was obliged to withdraw from under its cover and lie down a little to one side. Just at day-break, as I lay rolled in my blanket, something awoke me. Lifting up my head, there was a porcupine with his forepaws on my hips. He was apparently as much surprised as I was; and to my inquiry as to what he at that moment might be looking for, he did not pause to reply, but, hitting me a slap with his tail which left three or four quills in my blanket, he scampered off down the hill into the brush.

Being an observer of the birds, of course every curious incident connected with them fell under my notice. Hence, as we stood about our camp-fire one afternoon looking out over the lake, I was the only one to see a little commotion in the water, half hidden by the near branches, as of some tiny swimmer struggling to reach the shore. Rushing to its rescue in the canoe, I found a yellow-rumped warbler, quite exhausted, clinging to a twig that hung down into the water. I brought the drenched and helpless thing to camp, and, putting it into a basket, hung it up to dry. An hour or two afterward I heard it fluttering in its prison, and cautiously lifted the lid to get a better glimpse of the lucky captive, when it darted out and was gone in a twinkling. How came it in the water? That was my wonder, and I can only guess that it was a young bird that had never before flown over a pond of water, and, seeing the clouds and blue sky so perfect down there, thought it was a vast opening or gateway into another summer land, perhaps a short cut to the tropics, and so got itself into trouble. How my eye was delighted also with the redbird that alighted for a moment on a dry branch above the lake, just where a ray of light from the setting sun fell full upon it! A mere crimson point, and yet how it offset that dark, sombre background!

I have thus run over some of the features of an ordinary trouting excursion to the woods. People inexperienced in such matters, sitting in their rooms and thinking of these things, of all the poets have sung and romancers written, are apt to get sadly taken in when they attempt to realize their dreams. They expect to enter a sylvan paradise of trout, cool retreats, laughing brooks, picturesque views, balsamic couches, etc., instead of which they find hunger, rain, smoke, toil, gnats, mosquitoes, dirt, broken rest, vulgar guides, and salt pork; and they are very apt not to see where the fun comes in. But he who goes in a right spirit will not be disappointed, and will find the taste of this kind of life better, though bitterer, than the writers have described.

THE STILL
SMALL VOICE

One summer day, while I was walking along the country road on the farm where I was born, a section of the stone wall opposite me, and not more than three or four yards distant, suddenly fell down. Amid the general stillness and immobility about me, the effect was quite startling. The question at once arose in my mind as to just what happened to that bit of stone wall at that particular moment to cause it to fall. Maybe the slight vibration imparted to the ground by my tread caused the minute shifting of forces that brought it down. But the time was ripe; a long, slow, silent process of decay and disintegration, or a shifting of the points of bearing amid the fragments of stone by the action of the weather, culminated at that instant, and the wall fell. It was the sudden summing-up of half a century or more of atomic changes in the material of the wall. A grain or two of sand yielded to the pressure of long years, and gravity did the rest. It was as when the keystone of an arch crumbles or weakens to the last particle, and the arch suddenly collapses.

The same thing happened in the case of the large spruce-tree that fell as our steamer passed near the shore in Alaskan waters, or when the campers in the forest heard a tree fall in the stillness of the night. In both cases the tree's hour had come; the balance of forces was suddenly broken by the yielding of some small particle in the woody tissues of the tree, and down it came. In all such cases there must be a moment of time when the upholding and down-pulling forces are just balanced; then the yielding of one grain more gives the victory to gravity. The slow minute changes in the tree, and in the stone wall, that precede their downfall, we do not see or hear; the sudden culmination and collapse alone arrest our attention. An earthquake is doubtless the result of the sudden release of forces that have been in stress and strain for years or ages; some point at last gives way, and the earth trembles or the mountains fall.

It is the slow insensible changes in the equipoise of the elements about us that, in the course of long periods of time, put a new face upon the aspect of the earth. Rapid and noisy changes over large areas, which may have occurred during the geologic ages, we do not now see except in the case of an earthquake. It is the ceaseless activity, both chemical and physical, in the bodies about us, of which we take no note, that transforms the world. Atom by atom the face of the immobile rocks changes. The terrible demonstrative forces, such as electric discharges during a storm, which seem competent to level mountains or blot out landscapes, usually make but slight impression upon the fields and hills.

In the ordinary course of nature, the great beneficent changes come slowly and silently. The noisy changes, for the most part, mean violence and disruption. The roar of storms and tornadoes, the explosions of volcanoes, the crash of the thunder, are the result of a sudden break in the equipoise of the elements; from a condition of comparative repose and silence they become fearfully swift and audible. The still small voice is the voice of life and growth and perpetuity. In the stillness of a bright summer day what work is being accomplished! what processes are being consummated! When the tornado comes, how quickly much of it may be brought to naught! In the history of a nation it is the same. The terrible war that is now devastating Europe is the tornado that comes in the peace and fruitful repose of a summer's day. As living nature in time recovers from the destructive effects of the mad warring of the inorganic elements, so the nations will eventually recover from the blight and waste of this war. But the gains and the benefits can never offset the losses and the agony. The discipline and agony of war only fit a people for more war. If war is to be the business of mankind, then the more of it we have the better; if there is no true growth or expansion for a people, save through blood and fire, then let the blood and fire come to all of us, the more the better. The German gospel of war, so assiduously preached and so heroically practiced in our day, is based upon the conviction that there is no true growth for a nation except by the sword, that the still small voice of love and good will must give place to the brazen trumpet that sounds the onset of hostile and destroying legions.

Are the arts of peace seductive, and do they hasten the mortal ripening of a people's character? Must the ploughshares now be forged into swords and the swords used to spill our neighbors' blood? The current gospel of war is the gospel of hate and reprisal, of broken treaties and burned cities, of murdered women and children, and devastated homes.

What a noise politics makes in the world, our politics

especially! But some silent thinker in his study, or some inventor in his laboratory, is starting currents that will make or unmake politics for generations to come. How noiseless is the light, yet what power dwells in the sunbeams—mechanical power at one end of the spectrum, in the red and infra-red rays, and chemical power at the other or violet and ultra-violet end! It is the mechanical forces—the winds, the rains, the movements of ponderable bodies—that fill the world with noise; the chemical changes that disintegrate the rocks and set the currents of life going are silent. The great loom in which is woven all the living textures that clothe the world with verdure and people it with animated forms makes no sound. Think of the still small voice of radio-activity—so still and small that only molecular science is aware of it, yet physicists believe it to be the mainspring of the universe.

The vast ice-engine that we call a glacier is almost as silent as the slumbering rocks, and, to all but the eye of science, nearly as immobile, save where it discharges into the sea. It is noisy in its dying, but in the height of its power it is as still as the falling snow of which it is made. Yet give it time enough, and it scoops out the valleys and grinds down the mountains and turns the courses of rivers, or makes new ones.

We split the rocks and level the hills with our powder and dynamite and fill the world with noise; but behold the vast cleavage of the rocks which the slow, noiseless forces of sun and frost bring about! In the Shawangunk Mountains one may see enormous masses of conglomerate that have been split down from the main range, showing as clean a cleavage over vast surfaces as the quarryman can produce on small blocks with his drills and wedges. One has to pause and speculate on the character of the forces that achieved such results and left no mark of sudden violence behind. The forces that cleft them asunder were the noiseless sunbeams. The unequal stress and strain imparted by varying temperatures clove the mountains from top to bottom as with a stroke of the earthquake's hammer. In and about Yosemite Valley one sees granite blocks of the size of houses and churches split in two where they lie in their beds, as if it had been done in their sleep and without awakening them. This silent quarrying and reducing of the rocks never ceases to surprise one. Amid the petrified forests of Arizona one marvels to see the stone trunks of the huge trees lying about in yard lengths as squarely and cleanly severed as if done with a saw. Assault them with sledge and bar and you may reduce them to irregular fragments, but you cannot divide the blocks neatly and regularly as time has done it.

The unknown, the inaudible forces that make for good in every state and community—the gentle word, the kind act, the forgiving look, the quiet demeanor, the silent thinkers and workers, the cheerful and unwearied toilers, the scholar in his study, the scientist in his laboratory—how much more we owe to these things than to the clamorous and discordant voices of the world of politics and the newspaper! Art, literature, philosophy, all speak with the still small voice. How much more potent the voice that speaks out of a great solitude and reverence than the noisy, acrimonious, and disputatious voice! Strong conviction and firm resolution are usually chary of words. Depth of feeling and parsimony of expression go well together.

The mills of the gods upon the earth's surface grind exceeding slow, and exceeding still. They are grinding up the rocks everywhere—pulverizing the granite, the limestone, the sandstone, the basalt, between the upper and nether millstones of air and water to make the soil, but we hear no sound and mark no change; only in geologic time are the results recorded. In still waters we get the rich deposits that add to the fat of the land, and in peaceful, untroubled times is humanity enriched, and the foundations are laid upon which the permanent institutions of a nation are built.

We all know what can be said in favor of turmoil, agitation, war; we all know, as Goethe said, that a man comes to know himself, not in thought, but in action; and the same is true of a nation. Equally do we know the value of repose, and the slow, silent activities both in the soul of man and in the processes of nature. The most potent and beneficent forces are stillest. The strength of a sentence is not in its adjectives, but in its verbs and nouns, and the strength of men and of nations is in their calm, sane, meditative moments. In a time of noise and hurry and materialism like ours, the gospel of the still small voice is always seasonable.

NATURE NEAR HOME

After long experience I am convinced that the best place to study nature is at one's own home,—on the farm, in the mountains, on the plains, by the sea,—no matter where that may be. One has it all about him then. The seasons bring to his door the great revolving cycle of wild life, floral and faunal, and he need miss no part of the show.

At home one should see and hear with more fondness and sympathy. Nature should touch him a little more closely there than anywhere else. He is better attuned to it than to strange scenes. The birds about his own door are his birds, the flowers in his own fields and wood are his, the rainbow springs its magic arch across his valley, even the everlasting stars to which one lifts his eye, night after night, and year after year, from his own doorstep, have something private and personal about them. The clouds and the sunsets one sees in strange lands move one the more they are like the clouds and sunsets one has become familiar with at home. The wild creatures about you become known to you as they cannot be known to a passer-by. The traveler sees little of Nature that is revealed to the home-stayer. You will find she has made her home where you have made yours, and intimacy with her there becomes easy. Familiarity with things about one should not dull the edge of curiosity or interest. The walk you take to-day through the fields and woods, or along the river-bank, is the walk you should take to-morrow, and next day, and next. What you miss once, you will hit upon next time. The happenings are at intervals and are irregular. The play of Nature has no fixed programme. If she is not at home to-day, or is in a non-committal mood, call to-morrow, or next week. It is only when the wild creatures are at home, where their nests or dens are made, that their characteristics come out.

If you would study the winter birds, for instance, you need not go to the winter woods to do so; you can bring them to your own door. A piece of suet on a tree in front of your window will bring chickadees, nuthatches, downy woodpeckers, brown creepers, and often juncos. And what interest you will take in these little waifs from the winter woods that daily or hourly seek the bounty you prepare for them! It is not till they have visited you for weeks that you begin to appreciate the bit of warmth and life they have added to your winter outlook. The old tree-trunk then wears a more friendly aspect. The great inhospitable out-of-doors is relenting a little; the cold and the snow have found their match, and it warms your heart to think that you can help these brave little feathered people to win the fight. Not a bit daunted are they at the fearful odds against them; the woods and groves seem as barren as deserts, the earth is piled with snow, the trees snap with the cold—no stores, no warmth anywhere, yet here are

"these atoms in full breath
Hurling defiance at vast death."

They are as cheery and active as if on a summer holiday.

The birds are sure to find the tidbit you put out for them on the tree in front of your window, because, sooner or later, at this season, they visit every tree. The picking is very poor and they work their territory over and over thoroughly. No tree in field or grove or orchard escapes them. The wonder is that in such a desert as the trees appear to be in winter, in both wood and field, these little adventurers can subsist at all. They reap a, to us, invisible harvest, but the rough dry bark of the trees is not such a barren waste as it seems. The amount of animal food in the shape of minute insects, eggs, and larvæ tucked away in cracks and crevices must be considerable, and, by dint of incessant peeping and prying into every seam and break in the bark, they get fuel enough to keep their delicate machinery going.

The brown creeper, with his long, slender, decurved bill, secures what the chickadee, with his short, straight bill, fails to get. The creeper works the trunk of the tree from the ground up in straight or in spiral lines, disappearing quickly round the trunk if he scents danger. He is more assimilatively colored than any of his winter congeners, being like a bit of animated bark itself in form and color, hence his range and movements are more limited and rigid than those of the woodpeckers and chickadees. The creeper is emphatically a tree-trunk bird. His enemies are shrikes and hawks, and the quickness with which he will dart around the trunk or flash away to another trunk shows what the struggle for life has taught his race.

The range of the nuthatch is greater than that of the creeper, in that he takes in more of the branches of the tree. He is quite conspicuously colored in his suit of black, light gray, blue, and white, and his power of movement is correspondingly varied. His bill is straight and heavier, and has an upward slant with the angle of the face that must serve him some useful purpose. He navigates the tree-trunks up and down and around, always keeping an eye on every source of danger in the air about him. I have never seen a nuthatch molested or threatened by any bird of prey, but his habitual attitude of watchfulness while exploring the tree-trunks, with head bent back and beak pointing out at right angles, shows clearly what the experience of his race has taught him. Danger evidently lurks in that direction, and black and white and blue are revealing colors in the neutral woods. But, however much the nuthatch may be handicapped by its coloration, it far outstrips the creeper in range and numbers. Its varied diet of nuts and insects no doubt gives it a more vigorous constitution, and makes it more adaptive. It is the vehicle of more natural life and energy.

How winter emphasizes the movements of wild life! The snow and the cold are the white paper upon which the print is revealed. A track of a mouse, a bird, a squirrel, or a fox shows us at a glance how the warm pulse of life defies the embargo of winter. From cracks and rents in the frigid zone which creep down upon us at this season there issue tiny jets of warm life which play about here and there as if in the heyday of summer. The woods snap and explode with the frost, the ground is choked with snow, no sign of food is there for bird or beast, and yet here are these tiny bundles of cheer and contentment in feathers—the chickadees, the nuthatches, and their fellows.

FOR THE BEST IN PAPERBACKS, LOOK FOR THE

In every corner of the world, on every subject under the sun, Penguin represents quality and variety—the very best in publishing today.

For complete information about books available from Penguin—including Pelicans, Puffins, Peregrines, and Penguin Classics—and how to order them, write to us at the appropriate address below. Please note that for copyright reasons the selection of books varies from country to country.

In the United Kingdom: For a complete list of books available from Penguin in the U.K., please write to *Dept E.P., Penguin Books Ltd, Harmondsworth, Middlesex, UB7 0DA.*

In the United States: For a complete list of books available from Penguin in the U.S., please write to *Dept BA, Penguin, Box 120, Bergenfield, New Jersey 07621-0120.*

In Canada: For a complete list of books available from Penguin in Canada, please write to *Penguin Books Canada Ltd, 10 Alcorn Avenue, Suite 300, Toronto, Ontario, Canada M4V 3B2.*

In Australia: For a complete list of books available from Penguin in Australia, please write to the *Marketing Department, Penguin Books Ltd, P.O. Box 257, Ringwood, Victoria 3134.*

In New Zealand: For a complete list of books available from Penguin in New Zealand, please write to the *Marketing Department, Penguin Books (NZ) Ltd, Private Bag, Takapuna, Auckland 9.*

In India: For a complete list of books available from Penguin, please write to *Penguin Overseas Ltd, 706 Eros Apartments, 56 Nehru Place, New Delhi, 110019.*

In Holland: For a complete list of books available from Penguin in Holland, please write to *Penguin Books Nederland B.V., Postbus 195, NL-1380AD Weesp, Netherlands.*

In Germany: For a complete list of books available from Penguin, please write to *Penguin Books Ltd, Friedrichstrasse 10-12, D-6000 Frankfurt Main I, Federal Republic of Germany.*

In Spain: For a complete list of books available from Penguin in Spain, please write to *Longman, Penguin España, Calle San Nicolas 15, E-28013 Madrid, Spain.*

In Japan: For a complete list of books available from Penguin in Japan, please write to *Longman Penguin Japan Co Ltd, Yamaguchi Building, 2-12-9 Kanda Jimbocho, Chiyoda-Ku, Tokyo 101, Japan.*